MW01287224

Soul Dive

My Journey into the Deep

Alex Sabbag

Soul Dive

My Journey into the Deep

Alex Sabbag

Copyright © 2024 - Reflek Publishing

All Rights Reserved.

No part of this publication may be reproduced, distributed, or transmitted in any form or by any means, including photocopying, recording, or other electronic or mechanical methods, without the prior written permission of the publisher, except in the case of brief quotations embodied in critical reviews and certain other noncommercial uses permitted by copyright law.

Disclaimer: The author makes no guarantees concerning the level of success you may experience by following the advice and strategies contained in this book, and you accept the risk that results will differ for each individual. The purpose of this book is to educate, entertain, and inspire.

For more information: www.soulfulalchemist.com

ISBN (paperback): 978-1-962280-19-8

ISBN (ebook): 978-1-962280-18-1

Here's A Gift Before You Begin

I am honored to share Soul Dive with you!

Thank you so much for stepping *into the deep* and reading my story.

To receive FREE resources and bonus content please visit

www.soulfulalchemist.com.

Dedication

MBW,

There will be no one on this earth who loves me the way that you do. I know that somewhere in some realm our souls made a deal. And when I said in this earthly life I will need to learn who I truly am, you stepped up and said you'd show me the way. Through tragedy we've both been triumphant. There is always light at the end. Thank you for showing me the path to knowing who I really am. It is through our journey I found my voice and made this book a reality. You are a gift I will forever be grateful for.

With love and faith,

Alex

P.S., the answer always was and always will be, "Big ones."

A Note from the Author

I was in the early process of writing this book when my own father asked me,

"Why do you think your story is any different from everyone else's?"

Annoyed, I answered,

"It just is."

The truth is, it really isn't. My story is filled with the coming of age tales that repeat themselves throughout human history. They are stories of becoming, breakups, sorrow, and life handing me a ripe shit sandwich. Somehow, the end of every story is wrapped with a bow of grief and tied in light, humor, resilience and grace.

My lived experience has taught me more than any college education, fancy business school or wise uncle could. I've gained a lifetime of wisdom simply by waking up as *Alex* and walking all the days in my very own shoes. I've learned so much through my experience. I have had the dream of penning my own book since I was in my twenties. What started as a whimsical dating exposé has evolved into a personal story of reality and resilience:

"FROM TRAGEDY TO TRIUMPH," the headline would read.

In my twenties, I was too young to have lived enough life to give me a deep anchor for my own personal story. But now. . . now

I've lived through what I hope is the most traumatic experience I'll encounter in my lifetime, and I see things differently. The anchor I cast through that experience is less about what I went through and more about what came before and after. How did I get there and how did I get through it? It's valuable and worth sharing. No one reading this is immune to the fragility or questionable fairness that is life. Perhaps my story will both inspire and invite you into the flow of your own life with a little more ease.

The world needs real, authentic storytelling that shows us the way… Showing us the beauty through the pain, the rise from the ashes and the hope that rests when we anchor ourselves in faith. I'm not telling you how to live your life, simply sharing my experience. If, after reading this book, you leave with nothing else, know this:

1. **You are not alone.** While very few people on this planet have experienced what I have, most of us have encountered great loss and felt grief, sorrow, sadness, happiness, joy and delight. We can connect with each other through shared feelings and emotions. We don't all have to walk the same path to relate, to feel inspired or to show empathy.

2. **Don't stop living.** I took myself out of the ring of life for a long time, forcing myself to "heal" and expecting to emerge from my cocoon as a reformed person unmarked by all the things life had thrown at me. Know this—benching yourself isn't going to make it better. You do not have to be fully healed to be completely loved. The right people will love you through it. The ones that leave you are meant to go. Let them.

3. **You have to laugh.** My story is heavy, and at times gut-wrenchingly so sad I wonder why I'm so compelled to put it down on paper. But there is always an air of lightness that

aids in the delivery. My goal here is not to bring you to your knees. That may happen, especially if you are in the cycle of grief. If you do drop, give yourself grace, but more than that give yourself permission to laugh. Life is hard enough; we don't need to further punish ourselves by forcing a somber façade on the already heavily weighted world we live in. I will invite you into the light: Please join me there so we can continually be reminded what joy feels like in our minds, bodies and souls.

I consider myself a spiritual Christian. I am a two-time entrepreneur and currently own Soul Dive Yoga in Palm Desert, California. This is my personal story. It's anchored in tragedy and finishes with triumph. I want you to know you're not alone. I want you to feel seen, to experience connection and to rest easy in knowing that this life is for you. When you have faith, release expectations and surrender to God you will live the happily-ever-after: even though it may not look like you thought it would.

I hope as you read this book it feels like connecting with your best friend in her living room. It's deep, philosophical, hilarious, thought provoking and will fill your soul to the brim. My wish is this little tell-all leaves you inspired, lit up and better equipped to keep living with more peace, purpose and presence. Whether you're reading over a nice cup of tea or a few glasses of wine, my hope is that you too can connect with me through the emotions of my experience. We don't have to have the same journey to relate. My story was always meant to be shared. As I tap into the vulnerability of my life in all its painful, purgatorial and prophetic moments, through the grit and the glory, I hope you'll meet me there with love and grace.

Table of Contents

Introduction

I like to say there are two types of learners in the world: Those who get it the first time, Intuitive Learners, and those who don't, 2x4 Learners. You know those subtle taps? The gentle nudges from the angels, whispers from God and soft redirects from the universe? If you are an Intuitive Learner, one who hears those subtle invitations to see another path, live in greater purpose and choose more light, listen and respond, my hat is eternally off to you. But for some of us, myself at the top of this list, we aren't so responsive to *subtle*. You might notice the nudge, hear the whisper or feel the pull but you're not listening and certainly don't respond. 2x4 Learners ignore and keep pushing the rock up the hill. Yep, I see you because I was you.

Enter the 2x4 moment. The moment is where life slaps you upside the head, flattens you down to the earth and hits force quit on your world as you knew it—to the point you hardly recognize your own reflection in the mirror. Sound familiar? For good or bad, my highlight reel is chock full of these 2x4 moments. It seems I've been deaf, dumb and blind to the gentle guidance from my ethereal tribe and so the big guy has had to pull in the big guns and pummel me down to the ground until I finally wake-up. Over. And over. And over again.

My biggest 2x4 moment arrived on my 33rd birthday. It's not how I planned to spend the day, sitting in a hospital room waiting for a diagnosis that would change the trajectory of my life forever. This day was only the beginning of the journey I was about to embark on, but it is the most important part of my entire story. Without this 2x4 moment, I wouldn't have woken up. I wouldn't have been able to see the other path I should have been walking on, and would have been left, floundering in all the wrong directions. I hadn't been living in my purpose and it was only a matter of time before God upped the ante and served up a divine redirect so hard I couldn't see straight for a bit. As dramatic as it sounds, this was the only learning style I was accustomed to for the better part of my life. In other words, *it was normal.*

If you're reading this and berating yourself for not feeling the subtle taps, let yourself off the hook. You're in great company and in my experience, you can't quite get "there" without hitting the bottom. And the 2x4 moment is the catalyst to the bottom. You can't really have one without the other.

The 2x4 moments come in all shapes and forms: death, divorce, grief, abandonment, the unexpected job loss and sudden relationship fallout—the time where the door was so briskly slammed in your face it forced your body to ricochet. The landings are hard; it's nearly impossible to soften the blow of a 2x4 moment. And that's exactly why they exist. They are a force-quit, a divine reach down to lift you up and guide you back into your purpose: with a hope that the aftershocks are so strong you won't go back to the way things were. So you wake-up, eyes wide open and ears willing to listen.

We all have them because if I've learned nothing else, it is that no one—no matter the income, beauty or silver-spoon status—is immune to life creeping in and ripping the proverbial rug out from under their toes. The challenge you face begins with awareness, healing and pulling yourself up off the ground. The greatest challenge of all is to find gratitude for the fact that the moment happened to begin with—gratitude for your life before and your life after. That's the thing with these completely life-altering moments. You were who you were walking in, and in a split moment in time, the person you'll become after. I hardly recognize my 33-year-old self, and in fact, I'm pretty sure Alex 1.0 burned completely to the ground to make space for the 2.0 version you know today. And thank God for that. Thank God I found a path to surrender, to letting go and allowing so many layers of who I was to dissipate into the ether and make room. After experiencing all I have, I can tell you I finally feel a sense of peace and much gratitude for being dropped (or drop-kicked) into my purpose.

2x4 moments are exhausting, traumatic and leave us depleted and in need of soul-reviving life support. If we could simply slow down, tune in and listen, perhaps we could save ourselves from all the suffering. We will go through it, the ever-evolving change that life promises us. But if we can just let go, perhaps we could spare ourselves the dramatic turbulence along the way.

"Soul Dive" is defined as the period of time after my life altering 2x4 moment where I took myself out of the ring of life to recalibrate, heal and discover what in the actual F my purpose was. Your Soul Dive doesn't have to be years; it can be a moment, an hour-long yoga class, an afternoon or a vacation. Filed under *good for your soul,* it's an opportunity to slow down, regroup, go through, and re-emerge. Soul Dive is the name of my yoga studio in Palm Desert, California and serves as an invitation to come in, just as you are, and simply be. My journey into the deep brings soul dive over to a verb. It's biblical;

Jesus calls us into the deep. After living most of my life just below the surface, I found the bottom and had a glimmer of awareness of what it might be like to revisit life from the depth of my soul. It was no easy task. And would have been an impossible feat without the unconditional love and grace of God.

This book, *Soul Dive*, is precisely as it reads: my journey into the deep. It's my story of life as I knew it shattered in a split second and the painfully slow process of allowing it to completely burn to the ground. All of it. So I could rebuild and start living in purpose.

My journey into the deep forced me to sit in the painful purgatory of reaching the bottom with absolutely no clear direction of how or when I would begin to crawl my way back out. The deep is dark. Sometimes we're invited into the shit and asked to sit in it for an insanely uncomfortable amount of time. *Can we stay or do we run?* I ran so many times. I'd self-soothe by serial dating, putting so many proverbial bandaids on all the areas where I simply needed to just be, release and recover. But I didn't know how. I was never taught how to simply *be* in the darkest shadows of my life. I was always told to put my big girl panties on and get over it. If you were raised by baby boomers, you feel me.

I don't have a crystal ball, but I can tell you that the path of running from the shit will only lead to more and more 2x4 moments. Eventually you'll have enough of the soul crushing beat-ups and you'll wake up. I did, and I want to share my journey with you in hopes that you spend a little less time in your purgatory and more time inspired to live in your purpose. I hope you spend less time getting smacked upside the head and more time in surrender, less time in pain and more time in peace. Sitting in the shit is hard; it's dark, it stinks, we can't see, and we don't know how to get out. But the darkness is there for a reason and offers us an invitation to let an old part of ourselves die so we may find a new beginning. The darkness exists to show us the light.

The beginning. How beautiful. When people come to my yoga studio for the first time, they often ask,

"Where do I start?" The only answer I see suitable is,

"At the beginning of course!" By the end of the first page of Chapter 1, you'll know my 2x4 moment. I promise not to bury the lead. But remember, it's less about the moment and more about the reaction. It's the moment by moment, day by day process of surrendering, letting go and allowing your life to unfold the way it was always meant to be. Spoiler alert: this likely looks wildly different than your plan. It certainly did for me. So here's to all my 2x4 learners, all the stubborn, *me me me* agenda pushing A types out there who love talking about divine direction and absolutely refuse to surrender to God's plan. May your next 2x4 moment be your last. Life doesn't have to be this hard… It's a beautiful gift. Ready to know more? Let's start from the beginning.

Xoxo,
Alex (Your recovering 2x4 learner)

Chapter 1
The 2x4 Moment

The obstacles, the lessons and the divine redirects are the path.

June 16, 2018, on my 33rd birthday my boyfriend was diagnosed with terminal brain cancer.

24 hours prior I was wrapping up a vacation in Portugal and Spain with my best friend, Natalie. We spent ten days island hopping, indulging in God's Bread and sangria, fairly certain that upon our return, my boyfriend would propose.

When I boarded my flight from Barcelona to Chicago I received a text. My boyfriend was on his way to the ER. The next 24 hours unfolded as one of the most traumatic experiences of my life. Exchanging constant text messages along my nine hour flight back to the U.S., he insisted I go straight home to check on Alfie, my then twelve-year-old Yorkie, and get settled. The doctors did a CT scan and gave him a migraine cocktail, then sent him home. They said it was nothing major, just a bad headache.

I felt relieved. He had seemed off the entire time I was on my trip. He usually never complained, but was having headaches, issues with his vision, and couldn't sleep. When we FaceTimed, he looked pale and haggard. He was agitated, angry even. To say the least, he was not himself. I could feel in my bones that something wasn't right, but back then, I wasn't one to panic and certainly was not in touch with my intuition. I kept telling myself and him that it was stress: he was taking on too much at work and neglecting himself. These were normal things 40-somethings experience with demanding careers and new relationships. Everything was "fine."

One thing to know about me: I live for birthdays. The older I get the more I care, and I celebrate each one bigger than the last. At some point in my life I decided my happiness simply couldn't be left in anyone else's hands. If I controlled it then there was no one else to blame if things didn't go according to plan. (Oh how nice and incredibly naïve this theory was and still is.) I began my extravagant European birthday vacations just before my 30th birthday. I gallivanted around Italy, Spain, and Portugal. From the boyfriends to the beaches, my trips knew no bounds. I crashed bachelor parties in Barcelona, took a five-day vacation with an Australian in Ibiza, and downed countless cocktails with virtual strangers. It didn't matter the invitation: the answer was always yes. Risky? Maybe. But this was when I felt most alive, and my birthday was a catalyst to it all. The European holiday was my kryptonite. If I'm honest, it still is.

Going into my 33rd birthday, however, was a little different. I was in a relationship, which was a space I knew very little about. Even eight months in, it was fairly new for me, but I knew this time it was different. Just after two weeks of being together, we were in the back of an Uber and he asked me what kind of diamonds I liked. I had no idea, I didn't know what names to call the round or the square so I answered as truthfully as I knew how.

"Big ones," is what I told him, and oh my did he listen.

My birthday came the day after my return from Europe. A combination of jet lag and excitement pulled me out of bed early. I was relieved my boyfriend was okay and happy to be home, back with my person and ready to celebrate. We were on our way to the Soho House Chicago by about 8:00 a.m. where coffee, croissants, and frosé cocktails awaited us. Afterward, we would enjoy the early morning sunshine and a nice trip to the farmers market on the way home. We had the day planned, doing all of my neighborhood favorites before celebrating with my parents later that evening.

That year, my birthday fell on a Saturday. The next day was Father's Day, the day I was born. I had spent every single birthday of my life with my parents, and I didn't plan to stop the tradition this year. (How very only-child of me.) I wouldn't have it any other way. This year, the "Sabbag Party of 3" would have a fourth. I had longed for the day I would have my person at the table with me and my parents. Although I had told him a month ago not to propose, my dad tipped me off that he had asked for permission. I wasn't quite ready for the proposal— I wanted more time to just be in the relationship and allow it to unfold without the pressure of a wedding. This was the first serious relationship I had ever been in and the first time I had ever lived with someone. The love was there, but we needed a bit to sort out the little things. As much as we aligned, we still had different views about the necessary steps for post-dinner cleanup. I will retain to this day, the relationship just needed more space to develop. However, as time went on, I was prepared to accept his invitation should that be the way the weekend unfolded.

From the moment we met we were instantly drawn to each other. It was a soul connection. We came together and from the start things were serious; the relationship had a depth I had never experienced before. We celebrated his birthday just three weeks into knowing each other. We didn't just celebrate the day—I planned a week of things to do, ending it by falling asleep in each other's arms where he said, "I love you" for the very first time (but that, I didn't plan). He whispered the words so softly I wasn't sure if I dreamed it or if it was real.

But they were real, very real. He moved in a few months after we started dating. The co-mingling of his book collection, art supplies, hobby activities and meditation cushion took our relationship to a whole new level. In fact, one of my interns who really knew me and my level of OCD asked me,

"Do you want me to write this press release or organize his books?" I chose the latter, because as much as I loved him, I couldn't exist in chaos.

That morning, on my birthday, sitting up on the Soho rooftop, frosé and lattes in hand, was when he got the call. The ER department from Northwestern Hospital rang to tell us he needed an emergency brain MRI. This was not the invitation anyone is hoping for—birthday or otherwise. As a teaching hospital, scans are often read by residents and rechecked by the attending physicians. His CT scan was misread and someone caught it. I wondered from time to time, what would have happened if someone hadn't caught it? What if this unfolded like it does in China when the patient is not actually told they are diagnosed with a terminal illness? How would that have changed the trajectory of this story, of our relationship? Of my relationship with myself?

We made a beeline for the ER, waited hours for the MRI and more hours for the report. I will never forget the time waiting; it was the biggest purgatory moment of my life at the time. I know what I was wearing. I can feel the weight of the room and the intensity that existed between us as the fate of our future hung in the balance of Western Medicine. When the doctor finally gave us the news, within moments, the life that we thought we would have shattered. We couldn't quite believe or accept it. As we were sitting, waiting, we were also plotting. Already eager for a second opinion, someone to let us off the hook and make it all go away. As we sat in the stillness of impending chaos, there was no avoiding the truth. A match had been struck against the damp wood that weaved the fabric of ours lives together—and the future I had dreamed of living started to go up in smoke.

It was a *grade 3 anaplastic astrocytoma*, an inoperable glioma brain tumor pressing on the right side of his thalamus. To simplify, the tumor was more like an amoeba than a golf ball, and removing it would likely cause irreversible damage to his cognitive and physical function. He could end up paralyzed, not something a 42-year-old daily distance runner wanted to risk. The only thing clear in the early stages of the journey was this tumor would have to stay.

A brain biopsy was next, where the doctors would take a piece of tissue and run a genetic analysis of various gene expressions to dictate the roadmap for treatment. The biopsy couldn't happen for a few days and the doctors wouldn't let him leave. Despite the fact he never had a seizure, his doctor team put him on high seizure watch and restricted him to his hospital floor only. Funny how the system treats the sick like prisoners. It makes me ill to think that someone would be kept away from fresh air and sunshine, modern medicine refusing to believe in the healing benefits of simply being in nature.

Once he was admitted, my parents had made their way into town and the revolving door of hospital protocol began. Doctors, nurses, and social workers covered all the bases. I left to go home, pack a few bags and get Alfie settled with my parents at their hotel. I slept in his hospital bed with him the first night. The overnight nurses had no idea which one of us was the patient. He never presented as sick, so handsome, tan and seemingly healthy despite the debilitating symptoms.

The next day was Father's Day. I woke early, preparing to go back home to get more supplies. He insisted on me bringing his work bag. I was reluctant, thinking it was his job that brought on this whole situation to begin with. But I complied with the request, returning late in the morning with everything he asked for.

A few friends were on their way out when I arrived. Then it was just us. It was rare to get a moment alone in the hospital. Between the staff, friends and my family we were inundated with people in this tiny space. But moments after my arrival the space cleared and we were able to be alone for the first time since his diagnosis. We sat in the window and started to unpack the last 24 hours. The whole thing was new and so heavy, leaving us both riddled with anxiety and fear. We talked, but I can't remember what we were saying to process what was happening. I will never forget that somewhere in those moments the conversation shifted. He dropped down to one knee, taking my hands in his and telling me how much he loved me. He was an eloquent communicator, and he beautifully articulated how he felt, his love for me, his plan for us—our future. He asked me to marry him with the most beautiful ring I have ever seen.

I accepted. I had been waiting my entire life for a proposal. For years all I wanted to be was someone's wife. I longed for marriage, to be a couple, have a person, start a family and build a life. For a split second it seemed like that was the offer here. In some ways it was. Accepting his proposal quickly turned into plotting and planning. It was almost as if agreeing to marry him gave me the illusion of control that I could manipulate the matrix and we could bypass the entire tragedy we were served just 24 hours before. But in truth, it wasn't the moment of overwhelming joy my friend and I had been imagining. From that moment on, I had a front row seat to the painfully slow death of our future.

I became his primary caregiver. The proposal brought less feelings of everlasting love and light and more illusions of control. I fell abruptly into fight or flight. I had a title, a new job description. I walked brazenly into my new role as his fiancé. Alone we were powerless. Together, we were powerful. We had the connections, resources and now the time to figure this all out. He comes from a family of doctors, his brother's medical school buddy a radiologist in the Chicagoland area. The day of his diagnosis we put the disc with his MRI in the back of an Uber and sent it out for a second opinion. The woman who drove was no doubt an angel from God.

The opinion we awaited would hopefully empower, inspire and give us hope. The hope we needed to root down into the truth both of us so desperately wanted to believe. He was going to beat this, and come hell or high water I was going to make sure of it. But it didn't, the second read only confirmed what we already knew.

Within days of his diagnosis I placed my PR consulting company on ice. I had owned the business for about eight years at this point. As divine timing would have it, my number two was also checked into the same hospital giving birth to her second child. The leadership was quite literally pulled out of the business ring and checked into the infirmary for the time being. I called my twenty-year-old intern and offered her a promotion, which essentially was this: run the business, ask for grace, I don't care if we get fired. She not only kept every single one of our clients, but showed me how powerful it is to be passionate. I have endless gratitude for this woman and she knows I will always be the first to accept that reference call.

As everything was falling out around me, I kept going. I became the stepford wife of cancer caregiving. Emotionally void, all business and relentless until I knew he was saved. I was unwilling to accept what was really happening. It seemed the lens from which I was viewing my life was layered with delusion—I believed if there was a .01% chance death could be beaten, I was the woman for the job. And I wouldn't stop until I got us there.

At the time, it seemed the only choice was to assume the role of his caretaker, so I chose it. I chose to sacrifice my own life: business, personal and everything in between. I didn't have to, but if given the opportunity to choose it all over again I would still do it. The love we had was profound, an intense connection that felt other-worldly. Like we made a pact somewhere in the heavens that we would do this together. I believe our souls were destined to be together, and I do think to some degree I knew it wasn't going to be the beautiful love story I always dreamed would unfold. This had to happen first. His diagnosis changed the trajectory of my life forever. Being in the room, listening to the words leave the doctor's mouth void of emotion or human connection. A premature prognosis that these types of cancers could end his life in six months. It's like we knew well before any other testing came back. It wasn't good, the results just further solidified how bad it was.

We left the hospital a day or two after the biopsy procedure. My parents were still visiting and by now, his parents and brother had arrived as well. Discharge day is a waiting game. To prepare, our moms decided to go back to my house to get it ready for our arrival. The catch was this… his mother knew we were living together. My mother did not. We made the call to just let it unfold. And did it ever. My mom peppered her with many questions like why was his mail in my house, his clothes neatly assembled in my closet, so many personal items lying around. She fired away her opinions, judgements, and proverbial bullets so the gun was empty by the time we got home. Surprise! Just one of many that weekend.

When chaos ensues all you ever want is normal. I couldn't wait to get home, get back to some resemblance of normal. I was even half excited not to work, but also completely naive to what my new day-to-day life would look like. But there is no normal after a death sentence. There is life before and life after.

The first place I went after we were released was the yoga studio. I walked in, tears starting to stream down my face, as I was greeted by overwhelming excitement over my new (giant) engagement ring. I broke down, sobbing, telling the instructor my soul mate was dying. It was the first time I was given the space to lose it. So I did. Her response was one of the most powerful moments of my life. She didn't hug me, pity me, or *there there little girl* me. She gave me permission to enter the space however I was at the time—to come in and simply be. Take what I need, even if that means laying on my mat not doing one pose the entire class. Cry, scream, flail. The studio was my home and I needed to know I could arrive in any way, shape or form I was in at any given moment. What she did was empower me.

Up until that moment all I had received was sympathy. No one gave me permission to feel. And looking back, I needed that permission over and over and over again. It's impossible to feel when you're so consumed with fighting. Remember? I was tasked with beating death. Playing God. That wasn't the invitation here. It was at that moment the seeds of acceptance started to get planted. It didn't happen overnight, but I kept going, returning to the mat and to the room where I didn't have to fake it anymore. I didn't have to put on the happy face and tell the love of my life he was going to be okay. He wasn't, and we both knew it, but I didn't have the emotional maturity to sit in the darkness of honesty. I wish I could have. On the long list of regrets this is one of them. In hindsight I don't regret going through this painful experience. But I do regret not being able to get in the ring with him. I didn't have the emotional awareness and intelligence to admit I didn't know if we would be okay, if he would live or if we would end up with the life we both wanted. I didn't have the tools I do now. I lacked the ability to just be honest and hold space for the grief I know we both felt over losing the life we couldn't wait to live together. The dream was on the proverbial rug that was ripped out from under our feet and I was still trying to balance on the flying carpet in some alternative reality. *Real* was too hard. *Real*, at the time, wasn't an option. So I fought through control. Every single thing I could grasp, I did. I didn't know any better and in life we make do with the tools and resources readily available in our belts. The problem was, my belt was sitting empty on the shelf.

Yoga had always been a very physical experience for me. Like most, it was a way to get the long and lean body, stretch, sweat, and work out. That summer, yoga's higher power struck. The practice shifted from my primary form of exercise to my lifeline. I went as much as I could, pouring myself out on the mat and leaning into the harsh reality I didn't have power; I was forced into surrender. The lessons I was about to learn in life were showing up on the mat and I didn't even know it. Yoga has a profound way of finding you where you are. It did for me and without the established routine, community and commitment I'm not sure how I would have emerged from the darkness.

I promised not to bury the lead. So now you know. You know the moment that lit the match, the event that started the burn. And spoiler alert, you know I came out on the other side. It's not about the event, it's about where you go from there. While this experience anchors my story, it's not really the beginning. And as you know, all the great books start *In the Beginning.* . .

Chapter 2
Beginnings and Endings

Life prepares us for what's next: in order for something new to begin, something else must first end.

I'll begin where all stories do—at the beginning. Here's what we all have in common. We have stepped into this human suit to live on planet earth, and one day we will all die. That's it, friends. The rest is up to a blend of free will and fate. But we all start somewhere, and my beginning was with two incredible people who had no plans on having another child. Cindy and Allen were both on their second marriage, had adult kids and were ready to enjoy a beautiful new life together. However, fate had other plans and ten months into the union, my mom was pregnant. My dad was thrilled. My mom. . . not so much.

I am an only child, at least the only child between my parents, although I do enjoy the relationship of three half-siblings (who were almost grown by the time I was born). I became my mom's mini-me and was raised in a very adult world, given my brothers and sister were nearly twenty years older than me. We lived in West Des Moines,

Iowa, a classic suburban town. I did not grow up on a farm, milking cows and tending to chickens. When I meet people for the first time and share that I'm from Iowa I can see the farmtown fantasy scan their thoughts. Sorry to burst any bubbles, but this was not my reality. I'd love to have a farm some day and feel connected to that style of life. But alas, I lived in a beautiful house, had my own upstairs suite and never had to share a thing. The house had a big backyard, a pool, and two fireplaces frosted with my mother's elegant, eclectic style. I miss this house all the time. All of this is to say, I lived well.

When I was four, I decided I wanted to ride horses. My parents didn't think twice about my request. Instead, they booked a lesson and figured the whole thing would be too dirty or scary and I would bow out. The opposite happened, however: by the time I turned five I had a pony. Rusty the pony was my first ride. Then it was Fancy Angie, Mr. Chips (a moment for Mr. Chips and his lifesaving wisdom getting this chubby kid around a course when her glasses and helmet nearly flew off), Sebastian the dumb dutch warmblood, and then the prize, a gorgeous black thoroughbred named Monopoly who was one of the many grandsons of the famed race horse, Secretariat.

I was in all ways, shapes and forms the weird horse girl. My friends were largely from the barn, which is where I would spend most of my afternoons and evenings. My mom would pick me up from school, swing through a drive-thru so I could eat an entire value meal from whatever fast food joint we chose, and drop me off at the barn. I would stay for hours, making it home around 7:00 to then have dinner with my parents.

When I was home, I would create jumping courses in my basement with pillows, blankets and whatever else I could find. My friends and I jumped around the course like we were riding our own horses and after having enough of the running around, we'd force the dog over the obstacles, bribing him with treats. I still count in fours when I walk, because four steps is about equal to one stride. (When you walk the course in show jumping it's a best practice to know about how many strides the horse will take in between jumps.)

By middle school I was showing all over the country and competing against some big names (and even bigger money). I would leave school for extended periods, faxing in homework and doing worksheets and algebra assignments remotely. When I was younger my mom never missed a show. She went everywhere with me, and woke up at 4:00 or 5:00 in the mornings so we could get to the barn and prep the horse for the day, enduring the dust, heat and unforgiving elements often accompanying the show. Eventually though, to no one's surprise, she grew tired of the show travel and sent me along with the older girls who could drive. We were largely unsupervised outside of our trainer staying in the same hotel. As a result, I had my first beer at the age of twelve after a successful "hey mister" in a gas station parking lot in Mason City, Iowa.

Horses are magnificent animals and some of God's greatest teachers. Their grace, power and intelligence are unmatched. I grew up learning to communicate with these incredible creatures, and they became my friends. I would lay in the stall, knowing they wouldn't get up too quickly and harm me. We gave kisses and hugged. They knew me and cared for me. My horses taught me lesson after lesson in patience, the delicate blend of being soft yet powerful, and the embodiment of feeling our way through the dialogue and obstacles. There was no forcing the horse to do anything, and at any time I knew they could choose to toss me aside. I learned how to ask and to listen, developing my intuition with this unspoken communication between myself and my horse. Of course, part of all the learning is falling, which absolutely happened from time to time.

The worst of my falls was with Monopoly, who had a big personality and spicy temperament, along with a serious oral fixation. Monopoly was four when we bought him, and he was a bit green for my skill level, but had the pedigree and potential that fit my show circuit dreams and our budget. The day of the fall, we were in a clinic and he kept reaching back to chew on my stirrup. Then one time, just as he latched on, something spooked him and he pulled away, his teeth still caught. He flipped over on me, then freed himself and got up. I had a concussion and a broken thumb. In hindsight, we were both really lucky. That day I did what I always did, no matter how big the fall: I went back. My connection with these animals runs so deep in my soul, there's no doubt I was a horse girl in some way, shape, or form in all of my lifetimes.

The practice with my horse along with the pride in ownership and caring for these animals made me quite different from my peers. My sport was independent, reliant on an animal and my own guidance to direct us forward. I wasn't acquainted with team sports or athletics, and quite frankly was never really drawn to them. My dad attempted to get me into soccer, and I played for a season. During one game, I heard him yelling at me that I was running the wrong way. *Well, that was his opinion.* In fact, I knew exactly what direction I was running, and I shared with him that I wasn't interested in getting kicked. I was only there for the oranges at halftime. After just one season, I retired my cleats and shinguards and my dad gave up trying to get me to be anything but a horse girl. Horses were my passion and I was all in on competing. The only field I was interested in was a trail ride or grazing in the pasture.

I was always independent, a natural byproduct of being an only child. For good or bad, it took me years to appreciate solitude and release the loneliness of always being by myself. Growing up in the horse business allowed my independence to develop and gave me a skillset that youth team sports simply doesn't offer. I was learning how to communicate and build a relationship with another being that speaks an entirely different language. I was responsible for my role in my relationship with my horses and it was up to me to consistently work on building our connection. That was how we were going to be successful—together, as a team, the horse and the rider. It's the type of work you learn how to do when you enter an intimate partnership as an adult. It also came with the pressure that no one else was to blame if we failed. It was all on me. In a way, I've been learning and experiencing the grown up lessons of accountability since I was five years old and caring for my pony. Although I wouldn't trade growing up with my horses for a more "normal" childhood, there was a darker side to my being so independent. From childhood to my adulthood my mind defaulted to always doing things for myself, not asking for help and internalizing failure. The "it's all on me" mindset runs deep and while attributes of independence and big responsibilities are incredibly powerful for children to begin learning, my early years lacked a bit of the playfulness most kids have growing up.

Being raised by two older parents certainly had its perks. I had a luxurious lifestyle that set the bar high. I was given the chance to see the world and travel out of the country; London was the first stop at age five on a school Montessori trip. Outside of touring America's forgotten small towns for horse shows, my parents traveled often and brought me everywhere. I saw it all, grew up eating what they ate, and stayed in five-star hotels. My idea of childhood play was a game of backgammon with my dad's old real estate colleagues on his work trips. (I'm still owed ten dollars from one who may or may not still be alive.) Normal? Not quite. When I traveled for shows the only option was a Motel 8. But with my parents, the pattern was a suite with a baby grand piano. One summer, however, my parents decided to do something different and take a rafting trip to Moab, Utah. I was nine and this part of Utah wasn't nearly the upscale scene it is today. We drove through the Grand Canyon and made multiple stops to take in the view. Apparently I wasn't impressed. Never really one for the outdoors, this wasn't the travel I was used to. We arrived at the hotel and when my dad went to check in, I told my mom I wouldn't stay there. She asked why, and my response was:

"This isn't a Ritz Carlton."

My parents clearly raised a monster. Just ask any man that has dated me over the years. A simple weekend getaway really adds up once I weigh in on the accommodations. And while this is all true, I was a product of my environment. I knew what I knew and liked what I was used to. To put it delicately, adventure travel or outdoorsy experiences weren't really in my parent's vocabulary, apart from that one rafting trip in Utah. I will never know whatever inspired them to go rafting in Utah, but I can tell you it was the last of any nature-inspired family vacations.

Speaking the truth was imparted upon me from a very early age. This was an important lesson for me, and one that I hope we can all receive no matter how old we are. As we grow older, our voices dim and we can easily fall into the shadows of what we think we are "supposed to do" versus what we were put on this planet to do. *May I invite you back into your truth?*

My mother has shown me the way to live in my truth since I was a child. And clearly it stuck based on my demands for nicer accommodations. But in my acute awareness that I had older parents, a sense of fear started to develop in my system. My parents were old, and I was still young. I struggled to sleep as a kid. After we moved into our new house I felt fear, anxiety and what I would diagnose as my first awareness of loneliness. I begged my parents for a sibling. My dad would have done it, but my mom was a very hard pass. I remember struggling with this one night and, panic-stricken, ran down the stairs into their bedroom. My mom asked me what was wrong and I responded,

"You're old and you're going to die." My mom is an amazing truth teller. She said, "You're right, now go to bed."

That truth bomb right there started my journey of getting comfortable with death. Both of my parents have a beautifully unfiltered communication style. It's kind, but lacks any sort of sugarcoating in delivery. I was never really misled as a child outside of the usual offering to try this "chicken finger" when it was really calamari. I remember finding my baby teeth in my mom's closet while playing in her jewelry. We just locked eyes. The only thing I said was,

"I guess you're going to tell me Santa isn't real either." She calmly told me the truth.

The truth is one of life's most precious gifts and yet we avoid it. We let our truth sit on the bench while we placate popular opinion. This is what happened to me—the truth I learned with my horses somehow got put up on a shelf as I grew older. I wanted to fit in and be popular. I wanted friends and longed for boys to notice me. Here's the thing, I was chubby (borderline fat), had curly hair that my mother would brush until it turned into a ball of frizz (a form of child abuse we must bring to an end), glasses, braces and my mother's hand-me-downs as style. While I was logging hours in the barn, I was missing out on popular culture and normal kid stuff. I was aware of my weight but to my parents' credit, never insecure about it. I didn't really know any different because I was with my animals and not mallwalking and going into Spencer's with the cool kids. While I was somewhat blissfully unaware, my dad was not. I would pile ice cream into a bowl and my dad would take it away from me. My mom would yell at him that I would develop a complex, and then she would repeat the cycle of the fast food drive-thru before dropping me off at the barn, and then I'd return home to a big dinner full of meat, potatoes, and bread. I never missed a meal, and it showed. That's your good old midwestern values and a little meat on the bones.

My parents were established, happy and very much in love (and still are). I didn't know at the time how rare and special it is to be raised by two people who still love each other. My past is not full of darkness and this book is not the classic rags to riches memoir you may have expected. As I grew older and experienced some of life's challenges, however, I went looking for what could have been. I dug for trauma, thinking surely I was some kind of victim.

This searching forced me to confront the honest truth that I had a beautiful childhood. I hid it, often concealing where I lived thinking I would be judged. The older I got the less I let people into my home, or revealed my personal life. I hated the fact that I would be pegged as the kid with a silver spoon. It's almost as if having a traumatic experience as a child was the cool thing to do. It had to be there, the massive overcoming necessary to gain credibility and respect in our culture. I went down this path, wildly unsuccessful and frustrated that I couldn't join the masses in despair. I was upset, and resisted acknowledging everything I have in this life as a gift. Gratitude was nowhere to be seen. Instead, I punished my parents for their outdated opinions and failed to really accept the unconditional love and support they had given me since the moment I came into this world.

In ninth grade, my parents enrolled me in a private, Catholic high school. This marked my first experience as the *new girl*. It was also the time I started developing, growing not only taller than most everyone in my class, but also slowly shedding some of the weight, learning how to do my hair and consciously put myself together in the morning. I wanted to be pretty.

I never had a boyfriend in high school, but by the time I was a sophomore I started to notice and be noticed, mostly by older boys. I even went so far as to host a keg party while my parents were out of town because a couple senior boys thought it was a good idea. (They also left me with the hairdresser as a babysitter who was out having her own Friday night while I was home). Cue the eyeroll, I know. However, to this day, it remains a mystery how my parent's prized art-sculpture-cow split in two. More notably, one of the guys who brought over the keg remains one of my dearest friends. I will be forever grateful for the punishment my parents gave me for that party knowing that because of it, I've got him in my corner.

I wouldn't return to this period of time if my life depended on it. I'm grateful social media didn't exist, and that I wasn't even allowed to have a cell phone until I was fifteen or sixteen and learning how to drive. We were on the cusp of the digital era, but not quite all the way in.

I spent my high school days itching to go to college, get out of Iowa and experience real life as an independent reaching adult. I moved to Chicago when I was eighteen to attend DePaul University. I lived in Lincoln Park, joined a sorority and worked at a boutique on Armitage Avenue: I was a classic yuppy in training. While my dreams of a Lincoln Park brownstone might have since sailed away, the neighborhood will always have a beautiful place in my heart. Chicago became my home for the next eighteen years. I lived in different neighborhoods, evolved my friendships and built incredible connections—not to mention launched my first business at age 25—during my time there. Chicago is the second city to some, but it will always be the number one city to me.

I never thought I would leave Chicago. Whenever I would get an itch to go, something pulled me back in. It was comfortable, familiar, and accessible. I knew it so well that the city became my extended family. It's something I may have taken for granted until becoming the new girl again in a city across the country. Chicago facilitated my upbringing and showed me how to rise as a business owner, entrepreneur, mentor and accelerator. Chicago eventually pushed me out of my comfort zone and allowed the western winds to blow me away. I had learned all I could, and it became clear it was time for a change.

We love to talk about beginnings, but it feels unfair to do so without honoring the ending first. My farewell tour in Chicago in the fall of

2020 was one for the books—heck the police even came to my going away party after a noise complaint from a neighbor. Apparently they weren't so excited about the yoga session happening at 2:00 a.m. I had such a beautiful life there, one that was built over time, tremendous effort and plenty of tears. It would be unfair to think a new place could offer all that Chicago did for me in a fraction of the time. However, I knew when it was time to go. I prepared for my next chapter by letting go of what wasn't serving me in this one. I got rid of most of the contents in my closet, sold my furniture, and waited expectantly for what was next. Through all of this, I learned how to consciously and lovingly let go of my longest relationship, the city, looking back fondly and with great admiration for all it taught me.

It's so easy to celebrate new beginnings, but I'd be lying if I told you the fresh start in California was as blissful as it may have appeared on social media. The older you get the harder it is to be new, unfamiliar and disconnected. Starting over leaves so much room for the unknown. It's exhausting to think about even the smallest things, like which grocery store is on my way home! When we're young, there's a resilience in our beginnings. We practice over and over with team sports, new schools, extra curricular activities and following in the shadows of our parents as they navigate different circles, career paths and neighborhoods. When we grow older and choose to end a significant chapter in our lives, the weight of what's ahead is almost too much to shoulder sometimes. No matter how divine the new opportunity or path forward feels, we aren't immune to the challenges life has a tendency to throw our way. Moving cities and being the new kid gives us practice; it proves we can sit in some hard stuff. But the truth is, whether we invite the hard stuff in or are receiving it unexpectedly, it's still coming. I wasn't ready when it came for me.

Now, six years later, looking back through the trauma, the trials and the trek forward, I sit softly in the ready position. . . gently catching the curve balls and releasing the burden of them.

The rub with new beginnings is this: they simply aren't possible without the endings. You can't have one without the other. One chapter must end for a new one to begin. It's a cosmic law that proves its own truth time and time again. We can try to circumvent it, and like all things, there can be an exception to the rule. But for the most part, and from what I've learned, the ending is required before the beginning can take place. There was only one *in the beginning* (Genesis. 1:1, for those needing the reminder) and I'll be the first to admit, the liminal space between the beginning and the end, or the end and the beginning, is challenging to sit in and can be a little hard to decipher.

Whether physically, emotionally or energetically, we have to let go of what we are leaving before we can welcome in a new beginning. It can be helpful to look at it like a death. *So dramatic*, you may think, but that's precisely what they are. Endings are forms of death— they come in all shapes and sizes and have the potential to be both emotionally charged and energetically light. Endings are final. When we refuse to accept them, putting whatever scenario, from the career to the relationship, on denial's strongest life support, we are only delaying the inevitable from happening. By refusing to accept the end we cut the new beginning off at the knees.

We struggle with endings, and death for that matter, because we are afraid. We fear the solitude, uncertainty and loneliness that exists on the other side of so many endings. We fear what we don't know, we don't know because we haven't stepped into it, and we haven't stepped into it because we haven't ended the thing that had to come first. We can trick ourselves into thinking some of life's biggest pillars will just effortlessly flow into the next iteration without interruption. I not only see it all the time, I've done it. Like trying to get a new job while working overtime in the one you have, or attempting a new relationship when you're still committed to one.

The thing is, we so often struggle to end because we are unwilling to admit and accept death. So we stay stuck, kidding ourselves into thinking we can breathe new life into the failure and somehow things will change. What if we could stop the charade and just let it go? Let the thing die so we can start to process and actually have the space to call in the new beginning? New beginnings thrive on completion and spaciousness. You see, it's nearly impossible to admit and accept the ending because so often we don't feel complete. That's why we hang on and intubate the issue. A little force and a lot of control will change it! Nope, sorry. You're only delaying the inevitable.

Of course nothing is perfect. Maybe in an alternate universe where we're raised by AI and wolves we'll avoid screwing up our children and paying piles of money for therapy to repair the damage. But the truth is the truth: our humanness invites chaos, heartache and many imperfections. Our lives thrive through new beginnings, but the new beginnings need to know the old is complete; that it has ended, died and you're not still trying to bring it back to life. New beginnings can feel it, like an energetic frequency as powerful as when *you know, you know.* They can sniff out the resistance and know that you haven't quite let all the way go yet. My life had the appearance of perfection for many, many years. But no matter how privileged we are, we aren't immune to the challenges or 2x4 moments that inevitably drop in and shake things up. What we experience in life does prepare us for what's next, the beginnings, the endings and the liminal space between. And while we often don't even see it, we are divinely guided and protected along the way.

Chapter 3
No Immunity

*It's not about if life is coming for you,
it's when.*

One of the many problems with judgment is the assumption that if someone has certain things—money, beauty, or their dream job to name a few—then they are immune to life's difficulties. I've been the judge, sitting back thinking how perfect someone else's life is, wondering how nice it must be to "have it all." We've all been there, sitting in the *grass is greener* while the negative thought patterns bring self-doubt, scarcity and harmful dialogue to our own minds. But the truth is, we never have it all. No matter how lovely the façade, we are never fully healed, perfect beings. Again, remember what we all have in common. We are human. As humans, there is no perfect. If that's the hill you're currently dying on I'd like to invite you up and off it. It's a losing proposition. What's worse, the negative self-talk becomes so loud in your daily dialogue you start to believe it's real.

I learned first hand on June 16, 2018 I wasn't immune to the darkness life brings to the table. I wasn't immune to heartache, pain or grief. Being a good person with strong values, a great career, beauty, brains and all the other "things" that stacked my deck didn't grant me the pain-free life path. And so we are clear here, the person you think has it all isn't granted immunity either. It's just not how this matrix is set up.

While my youth lacked any serious trauma, I wouldn't exactly say it was without struggle. I experienced a few bouts of bullying, my first in junior high. I was accused of stuffing my bra. Truth be told, I probably was doing that and anything else to try and look like I had some kind of a womanly figure. Kids are mean, but this wasn't even the half of what I would later encounter. By my junior year in high school I was constantly bullied, mostly by a group of boys in my grade. They harassed me with phone calls and called me names in the hallway, each one more demeaning and cruel than the last. They targeted my house with pranks, and my so-called friends became unreliable, distant and more likely to hang with the mean kids than with me. This kind of treatment is disgusting. It lacks respect and kindness. Things got so bad the principal asked me if I would like a few of them expelled. What a weight to place on a teenager's shoulders. The school system failed me then, as it fails so many kids now, refusing to stand up to bullies and their parents. We owe it to our kids to be better and to protect them and show them that this kind of behavior isn't tolerated.

I've always been aware of others' perception of me. I never wanted anyone to think I had a silver spoon, or that my dad has made my career path possible. The thought of that eats me alive. For some reason (oddly enough my deep self-work hasn't uncovered the why here on this yet), I've cared so much about what other people think

I completely lived my life according to how I thought I should show up in the world. *What will the guys I'm trying to date want me to be like? How should I act to be accepted by this group of people?* You wouldn't think someone with as much independence and confidence would be this way. That's the trouble with perception: We assume. So I assumed, because I was raised a certain way and life came relatively easy, I needed to work that much harder to gain my credibility.

So I did. I curated a life in Chicago that had the "she has it all" façade. Kudos to me because I nailed it. I had a beautiful home, was well heeled, fit, seemingly healthy, and had a vibrant dating life. It was only a matter of time before Mr. Right came on the scene! I can see it so clearly now, what I couldn't see then: The veil of perfection I placed delicately over my own fragile shoulders. I wonder how often I was really myself? How much of my life was actually serving my soul? I can tell you it wasn't much. If I had lived for myself, done the life-giving things that filled me up and surrounded myself with people who amplified my life, I would have leaned into the subtle taps and maybe, just maybe wouldn't have had to suffer through the trauma I experienced through my fiancé's diagnosis. Remember? I'm a 2x4 learner. The subtle taps just weren't working. So I kept going, further and further out of alignment with who I was put here on this earth to be. I lived for expectations. Expecting my life to be at a certain point because I was "that age" or lived in a certain neighborhood. I spent so much time expecting things to happen I wasn't actually living in a way that would welcome them into reality. *Disconnected* is the word that comes to mind.

The thing about expectations is when we have them we are essentially talking ourselves into a reality that isn't here. Expectations hogtie our happiness to a certain outcome. Maybe it's already coming, or maybe we are forcing it, I don't know. But what I do know, and what was especially true for me, is when life goes in another direction than we expected, we fall apart. We not only lack immunity to the shit hitting the fan, we are mostly void of any coping mechanisms to take us through the storm.

I know this to be true because I've been there. I sat in a tiny room in the ER with my boyfriend, awaiting news that would change the trajectory of our lives. Once the news hit, my fight or flight took over (and didn't let go for upward of six years). To this day I am still actively healing my nervous system. I didn't know how to receive information and simply breathe. I didn't know how to hold my person and admit that things were not going to be okay for the foreseeable future, but he wasn't alone and we would navigate it together, as a team. I bulldozed right past the reality of the situation and all the feelings that came with it and sprang into control. Why? Because I expected my life to be a certain way. And I refused to accept that it wasn't.

I had no tools because I wasn't taught. I was (*ahem*, and still am) young and I wasn't raised in a household that was really big on navigating feelings. To no fault of my parents, they taught me what they knew; they were straight out of the bootstrapping baby boomer era. "Dust yourself off and get back out there" was their life's motto. I hadn't yet soaked up the knowledge from my yoga practice and my peers were on the same vibration as I was.

My life was just *fine*. Nothing was wrong with it and as much as I communicate that I was living outside my purpose, it wasn't a harmful mess. It was *fine*. *Fine* is acceptable to most. And I fell into that category for a long time. I settled for things being just okay, thinking,

Hey it could be worse!

So I stayed complacent in my own world. Complacency is the pipeline to death. Stay complacent and you reject growth. Reject growth and you only have one way to go: six feet under. I absolutely despise complacency and I lived it for years... and years... because it was simply easier to stay. And if you were the observer, looking at the life I built and spent so much time and energy forcing to be the way I expected it to be, you'd see a beautiful woman in her early 30's who had it all. I know how it looked. It's precisely why the judgements are so dangerous. The outside and in of my world wildly disconnected, hiding behind the veil of perfection.

The Bible tells us we aren't held accountable for what we do not know. Good news for me as I knew absolutely nothing, outside of the fact that I had some delusional illusion of control. I only knew grief by losing a grandparent. Sad, but different. I knew pain from the many breakups I had experienced over the years. This still was a far cry from watching my future go up in flames. I had yet to experience something this earth-shattering and I was so disconnected from my emotions I immediately spiraled into the assumption that no one could relate. I was alone, and only had me to navigate us out of this crisis.

Hello God, can you hear me?

After the diagnosis, my home became our cancer's grand central station. A revolving door of people showing up to help, keeping him company and offering what they could to support us. My home was hijacked of the serene sacred space once held and left me feeling displaced, isolated and empty. One of the only places I felt comfortable going was the yoga studio because people didn't know what was happening in my life. I was just another body sweating through a vinyasa class. I felt supported and empowered so I kept coming back.

Brené Brown defines empathy as the emotion that underpins the experience. I love this explanation. The people who show up for you in life's darkest moments don't need to have the same experience. If you love them, then you hope they never experience what you're going through. The sixteen-year-old going through her first break-up is feeling the same sadness and grief as the 40-year-old woman going through the divorce. We aren't so different, and we don't need to understand through the same experience to really get it. I wish I knew that then, so I share it with you now.

So there I was, 33 years-old, with a can of gasoline in one hand and a lit match in the other. Of course I didn't know it at the time. If we define knowledge as lived experience then it's quite simple to say I had no knowledge of what to do. And if wisdom is knowledge applied, then I was the furthest thing from wise someone could possibly be. I didn't really understand the difference between sympathy and empathy. I reacted and went full blown mama bear on the situation, thinking the more obsessive I got in the details, the more I could control the outcome. In hindsight, it was naive and at the core, both me and the situation were extremely sad.

In life, the question begs: Do we really need to go through the pivotal moment in order to be ready for the next one to hit? Do we need to contract all of the emotionally turbulent viruses so our bodies can recognize when tough times are about to strike? I don't think so. I actually think we can, and should get ready, and be ready, for whatever it is we need to be ready for. Just because you aren't immune doesn't mean you need to sit idle waiting for the next shoe to drop. This is where your tools come in. While nothing could have fully prepared me for what I was stepping into, the role of caregiver, I certainly could have had some things in place that offered a softer landing. It wasn't until later I realized how essential it is to have a practice. I didn't really have it then. I had a wish and a prayer that the whole situation would just go away overnight.

I have to tell you the truth. The question is not *if* life is coming for you, it's *when*. It's through the grit we find the glory and in the burn we're able to enjoy the bounty. None of us, not even the ones who have it all, are immune to riding the waves of life during our time on earth. No one. And when the biggest waves hit, sometimes we take a fall from grace. It's not because we're singled out by the Universe or being bullied by God. It's because we need to reach the bottom. It's the physical and spiritual force-quit on your life as you knew it that follows the 2x4 moment, leaving you flat on the ground so that you have no choice but to leave who you were behind and rediscover who you're put here to be. The bottom is hard, it's lonely and it's sure as hell the most difficult time I've yet to live in my life. Arriving at the bottom gave me one thing I'll forever be grateful for: the awareness that life was never going to get any worse than it was right then and there.

Chapter 4
The Bottom

The bottom is a beautiful place to be once you realize you've arrived, and things can't get any worse than they already are.

I was in the throes of caregiving for my fiancé come July of 2018. The decision to start standard of care was made, which meant my life was consumed by daily radiation, a chemotherapy protocol, regular steroids and other condition-managing therapies. I was Mission Control. I had the schedule, knew the dosage and absorbed the aftershocks of what all of this brought to our table. To say the least, it wasn't pretty. There is nothing particularly uplifting about logging hours in the bowels of the hospital or the mask he had to wear that could have easily doubled as a costume in an upcoming Halloween movie. No matter how much the system tries, there is arguable dignity to maintain by anyone going through the process, patients and their families alike.

But there we were, in it. We had six to eight weeks of high intensity therapies to do whatever we could to stop, or slow down, the growth and mutation of the tumor. Any type of cancer therapy is brutal, but there is something particularly unfair and challenging about the brain. The manipulation caused by the cancer itself was one thing, but the methods used to treat it another. The constant swelling and need for steroids, looking back, is one of the cruelest things you can do to a person. His body was pumped full of chemicals that caused extreme rage, amplifying the fire already stoked within him. But the steroids were necessary to reduce the chance of seizures, endure the treatments, ensure the body felt hunger and could muster the energy for basic human function. He was so exhausted at the end of every treatment that he slept for at least three hours when we returned home.

There is a lot about how I showed up during this time that I've since needed to work through. One of the biggest was my inability to really sympathize with what he was going through. I never allowed myself to slow down and sit with his feelings, or mine for that matter, and really observe what our life had evolved into. I know he could have met me there, emotionally; he had the greater capacity of understanding emotions, sitting with what is and being in uncomfortable feelings. But I was a total newbie.

The man had some serious depth, it was one of the things I found most attractive about him. Although I found his depth attractive, when we first got together and I learned about his meditation practice I was a little spooked. I wasn't there yet; I didn't know the true intention behind the practice and I let other uneducated voices get in my head about it. Meditation wasn't something I had much exposure to, and needless to say the mindfulness movement wasn't so prominent in Iowa where I grew up. It was new, a bit foreign and up until this relationship hadn't made it into my living room. I was face to face with meditation and hadn't had enough experience with it in order to truly understand the importance and benefits of the practice. When we moved in together, we fought about the placement of his meditation cushion. There were times where, when we'd fight, I would weaponize his daily practice, blaming him for the fight and telling him maybe he needed to spend more time *sitting*. Our relationship never really had the opportunity to hack out this kind of stuff. He was ready to teach me about meditation, mindfulness, and the beauty of silence as intimacy. In part, I wasn't ready to learn. We were connecting, and while our relationship did go rather quickly, we weren't given the gift of time to truly understand each other's beliefs and practices. Oh how I wish I could learn from him now.

When you're smack in the middle of chaos like we were, the connection suffers. I know he needed more of my emotional support, but I lacked the understanding of how to go there. Instead, I was operating from fight or flight and just kept going. It's all I knew, and after years of learning and reflecting, it wasn't a healthy way to manage our shared situation. I'm the first to admit the "keep going" approach was the most destructive thing about being in fight or flight. I didn't see what was happening because my adrenaline was driving this illusion of control that if I could just do a little more, I could alter the outcome. Back then, I believed that telling us there wasn't much we could do put his feet prematurely in the grave. So I didn't listen, instead I pushed for an unrealistic outcome. I kept forcing him to live, instead of accepting that so many parts of us were dying.

In China, when a person is diagnosed with a terminal illness it is culturally appropriate not to tell the patient. In over 80% of cases, when the family requests it, the doctors do not inform the patients of their condition. I think this is utterly fascinating and a beautiful way to allow the patient to connect with their body and make their own decisions—outside of the influence of western medicine. I wholeheartedly believe in the body's innate power to heal. And my fiancé was in the best possible shape to do so. Not only from a physical standpoint, but his meditation and devotional practices were the strongest of any human I've met to date. He was ready to teach me things my former 3D self couldn't wrap my dense brain around. The second you hear "terminal" while sitting in a sterile white room with some emotionally void voice in a white coat delivering all kinds of clinical messages you don't understand, well all you really hear is *I'm dying.* All I heard was a challenge to defeat all humanly possible odds. I'm not sure he really heard anything. So on this one topic, I think China is on to something.

What we needed, and really what I needed, was hope, and a healthy sense of normalcy to avoid creating the downstream issues that so often come with a major trauma and/or illness. I certainly didn't get that from the hospital setting. And let me tell you, I'd like a comment card from that institution. I could write a separate book on what quality care and personalized medicine actually means. It's certainly not what you think. When I asked about diet, knowing we had resources and could get whatever it was that would help his condition, the feedback was to just keep doing what you're doing. I pushed further, asking what they would advise someone living on the South Side of Chicago living on food from a bodega should do. I got the same answer. The truth is, these globally recognized cancer care teams don't know much about the body. They know about the disease, yes, and they have developed wonderful therapies to eradicate many harmful strains. But they don't really know how to treat the body for true optimal health.

As the person responsible for the health and wellbeing of their patient you would think the care team would take more time to listen to me. While my mind was definitely altered during this point in my life, it wasn't receiving daily laser beams; his was. I had a clear understanding of the reality of our daily life. I also knew that whatever was happening to my person was starting to affect me and our household and it was about much more than the cancer. The person I fell in love with had a gentle softness that I adored. The person I was now sharing a home with was enraged and unpredictable. I didn't know how much of this was the cancer, the treatment, or our situation. The highs and lows, the mood swings, the anger: All of it understandable, and I did understand. But the conditions we were living in were uninhabitable at times and my emotional wellbeing was spiraling. There were days I didn't feel safe in my own home—not necessarily physically unsafe, but emotionally. We weren't even halfway through the standard of care process before I realized this.

I attended most appointments, tagging out only when his family was in town. I would share what life was like at home, offering my perspective on his condition, quality of life, patterns of behavior and more. I was not engaged to a harmful man, nowhere near. But these medical interventions and therapies were taking away the person I fell in love with and leaving an angry shell of a human behind. Was this him or was it his cancer? At the time I wasn't sure. We were only together for about eight months before he was diagnosed. I felt like things were crumbling so quickly. I didn't have a big enough sample size to make that assessment prior to being in the moment when I needed the character account.

I asked the care team for help. Was there something else they could give him? Could he stop the steroids? Could they alter the protocol so that I wasn't pinned against the wall with him screaming at me multiple times a week because he was unable to control his brain? The responses were appalling. They referred me to a social worker, and then a therapist who was about 24. From the look on her face when she listened to me tell her I was taking care of my fiancé, less than a year into a relationship, who was fighting terminal brain cancer, it may as well have been day one on the job. I persisted. Even if you take me out of the equation, his quality of life was not great and it was my job to advocate for him—for us. More than once, our main nurse—the right hand woman to the most famous brain cancer doctor at this institution (and possibly the world)—asked me to leave the room. Why? Because it wasn't about me.

Mic drop.

You learn a lot about a system when you're in the thick of it. If you think for one second the cancer, terminal or otherwise, is only about the person living with the tumor, you have wildly underestimated how destructive the disease is to begin with. I was completely unsupported from a medical perspective and because we weren't married, taken even less seriously. The lack of respect (in my case) and overall support for me as a caretaker was abysmal. When I tell you it requires an army to care for someone going through a terminal diagnosis I mean it, and the medical team is only a small part of that. I am a fighter. (If you didn't grab that from the 2x4 moment piece, note it here.) When fight or flight struck, I doubled down. I didn't take no for an answer and I certainly didn't fight fair. I couldn't. You will lose every single time in the medical system if you sit back and "yes doctor" about your condition. I have no medical degree, but I was up close and personal to one of the deadliest and hardest to treat cancers out there.

I am fascinated by how life prepares you for what you're about to step into next. I had no idea my consulting business was doing just that. At the time we were battling cancer, I owned a boutique PR company that supported nonprofit organizations with communications and fundraising. A lot of my clients were in the healthcare and cancer research space and I was recently wrapped up in a communications program around customized treatment for gastrointestinal cancer patients. Through this project I learned that *personalized medicine* means that the tumor is analyzed for a series of genes experts deem relevant and important for that type of cancer. The genes are either expressing or not, present or not (my simple words, not a clinical definition here). This is a very elementary way of breaking it down. What this does not do is take into account anything about the person. Where they live, what they eat, who cares for them, hobbies, etc. Nothing. It's analyzing genes. We all have 22,000 genes in the body—file that under our humanness commonality—and cancer specialists have indicated roughly fifteen to twenty matter per cancer. These reports provide a roadmap for treatment (or so they say). Certain results may tell you the tumor is very responsive to chemo, slow growing and easy to shrink. Others may tell you the tumor is highly aggressive, resistant to chemo and standard of care may only temporarily slow it down. The latter was our report.

Nothing in the analysis or crafting the path forward looked at him as a person. The decision to do standard of care was going to be made no matter what; it was like the genetic evaluation was more connected to prognosis than determining what protocol to use. Remember this is only my opinion, and I'm not a doctor. But when pressed (which they really don't like) I was not hearing anything specific, simply blanket statements like,

"Keep doing what you're doing."

Should the low income patient who eats fast food all day keep doing that? Come on... even four hours of nutrition training tells you otherwise.

I've had a lot of bitterness to release about my experience with the care team, and a fair amount of trust to rebuild on the doctor front as well. This won't shock you, but working with naturopathic practitioners, alternative medicine providers and true healers offers the holistic approach I think anyone achieving optimal health might want to consider. There are affordable practitioners and methods that defy traditional medicine. I am not a doctor and this is not medical advice, but from my experience and what I know about the human body, alternative routes coupled with traditional therapies are the best course of action.

So there we were. It was late July, and we were full throttle on the treatment that may or may not do anything for the cancer at all (meanwhile wreaking havoc on the life of one of the most incredible men I've been blessed to know). I wonder if he wasn't influenced by his doctor if he'd choose to go through all of the therapies again? But in this reality he did—we did. Things got pretty dark in our world. I was unqualified for my new role as caretaker yet continued to pour my heart and soul into trying to save him. Everything shifted on to my plate: his care schedule, appointments and leisure activities all needed scheduling: preparing his friends for how to take him on outings, everything... including, on a lighter note, our subscription to Imperfect Produce.

Imperfect Produce is a subscription to receive the less attractive produce by mail. Think ugly carrots and bumped apples. Still delicious, just a little flawed. I logged in to customize our next order (my first time doing so) and made my selections. A few days later about twenty boxes arrived at my house. It looked like a weekly delivery for a restaurant! Conveniently, my parents arrived that afternoon as well. My mom and I unboxed the most massive amount of fresh produce I've ever seen. I had no idea how I ordered so much... until I revisited my account and realized that what I thought was pieces was really pounds. Four blood oranges? Nope, four pounds. Plums? Pounds. And so on...Apparently I don't read the fine print.

I can't stand food waste so my mom and I went to work chopping, juicing and prepping it all so it could somehow be used. We also gave quite a bit away. I will never forget this moment. You know in the midst of all the chaos and darkness that was surrounding my existence, the moment of handling twenty boxes of unexpected produce was like the moving meditation my mind, body and soul really needed. While I am forever grateful, I did cancel my subscription citing lack of trust in myself to properly provide for the lovely produce that arrived.

Our downstairs neighbors were big recipients of all our extra goods. They were also hanging on to all of my alcohol, which I had removed from our house a few weeks prior to avoid any dark moment of temptation. It was there. And I can tell you mixing bourbon and steroids is a lethal combination.

One weekend, my parents arrived to visit for a few days when my dog Alfie went racing toward my mom as she entered the apartment. Alfie ran toward her on the couch, leaped, missed, and fell back on his neck. He screamed in pain, something I had never heard him do. I had often worried about him and his place in our now new normal. He had an amazing bond with my fiancé and was becoming a huge fan of the daily afternoon naps. But he was small, sometimes in the way and living with a person who didn't have full function or control over his mind and body. For a small creature who was used to having only me around this was a sizable shift. That weekend of his fall, I guess you could say the other shoe dropped.

Alfie was in excellent health prior to this accident, but after this fall he started limping around. No matter what I tried, I couldn't soothe him or get him comfortable, so I took him to our neighborhood vet for some imaging, which returned nothing serious. I had him in bed with me that night, per usual, and he woke up crying again. I gently grabbed him to try and make him comfortable and he bit my thumb pretty aggressively. He only had half his teeth at this point, so the bite wasn't bad, but it let me know something was very wrong. I checked him into an ER for MRIs and other testing. They returned mostly normal: he had injured his neck, but nothing was broken. The veterinarians couldn't find out what was wrong. By the end of the night, my dog also had a team of neurologists. You really can't make this stuff up, can you?

Alfie was put on bedrest. There was to be no running, no jumping, and no activity outside of going to the bathroom and eating. He was an extremely active dog so this was torture for all of us. He also hadn't been in any sort of confinement since he was crate trained as a new puppy, so his new bed on the ground didn't exactly thrill him and broke my heart into so many pieces.

My reality was looking pretty grim. The daily radiation and chemo protocol was starting to take a really big toll on my fiancé. And now the dog, well... that put me over the edge. I was running a high class infirmary and I think the one that needed the most triage was me. I had a lot on my plate between these two and I am grateful the yoga studio was just around the corner. I tried to go every day. It was the only thing that made me feel somewhat normal—a little vacation from my life that just kept getting worse.

Even though I had yoga, I still felt defeated. One afternoon I made my way down to our neighbor's apartment, carrying Alfie in one arm and an empty glass in another. I needed a blood orange margarita. Afterall, only three pounds of them were freshly squeezed, ready for mixing. My kind neighbors whipped up a cocktail with my ingredients and I took it to the tiny patch of grass just behind my building. I gently placed Alfie down and took a seat on the little wrought iron fence that surrounded the area. It was partly in the alley, and partly on the sidewalk. I was there often, and actually given the amount of time it took Alfie to do his business I started making other friends in the neighborhood. I sipped my cocktail and watched my little furbaby hobble around the grass. His injury wasn't life threatening, but he was in pain, which hurt my heart.

I sat there at that moment thinking about everything that was in my life. . . The facts, the truth. I scanned through a list. I had finally gotten the thing I wanted the most, which was a proposal to be someone's wife, and look at where that landed me. My world was crumbling, piece by piece. My person was dying, my dog was injured, my career—the company I worked so hard to build—existed but with no place for me. My home was hijacked. My friendships were dissipating. The people around me were trying to help, I believe that. But I couldn't connect. I was being pitied and what I needed was to be empowered. I have had an incredibly blessed life and will be the first to admit it. But this was dark. All the things that used to fill me up were being taken away—my friendships, career, independence and the possibility that I would find love and start a family. At that moment I realized I was at the bottom. I was unable to sugarcoat the current reality or convince myself that it would all be okay. Nothing was okay, starting with me. I was a shell of the person I had been a few months prior. I hardly recognized myself in the mirror. The only thing shining about my being was the enormous ring placed on my wedding finger. I had been given everything I wanted and now I was watching the painfully slow burn of my future make its way down to the ground.

What I lacked in tools and coping mechanisms I made up for in awareness. I have always been acutely aware of everything: people, energy, perception. Often, I find myself finishing a sentence in my head before someone can get the words out. I've always just *known*, but never known how or why. This moment was no different. I knew I was at the bottom. I knew that there wasn't anything else that could be taken away from me that would hurt worse than what was being ripped from my tightly gripped fingers at that moment. Losing a parent wouldn't even be this hard. My future, the life I wanted to build, the family I was ready to start: it was all up in flames.

The thing about arriving at the bottom is that you'll never really know how long you'll be there. I do firmly believe having awareness of the arrival is huge. I knew with every cell in my body I was there. But that's about all I knew. I didn't fully understand the match was in one hand and the gasoline in the other. I didn't know I'd be there for as long as I was. I didn't know everything I knew would burn to the ground. And I didn't know how I would get out. I just knew I would. I knew the right opportunity would come along and I would take it, putting one foot in front of the other to heal and rediscover why I'm here. That awareness wasn't present, but I knew enough about the rules of the cosmos in that everything is fleeting and we won't be in the same place forever. Thank God. Forever is a very long time.

Acknowledging that I had arrived at the bottom almost gave me comfort. It's like thinking, *Okay, nothing else can fall out that hasn't already gone.* I was able to wrap myself in the security blanket of solace knowing things really couldn't get any worse. It also gave me a break from the fear of losing something else. I think the only thing worse than actually losing someone you love to death is watching, and that painfully slow process of the person you love slipping away. That was me. I was sitting in the VIP field seat witnessing my own life game play out in the opponent's favor.

This was when I came to realize another hard truth. I was not only bottomed out of my life, but the person I had always known for 33 years was fading away. I was also dying. Metaphorically speaking, Alex 1.0 was on her last leg. The life I had envisioned for myself was vanishing. It became clear I needed to make a decision. Was I going to put myself on life support and keep living for some dream that I had to force into reality? The dream of being married, having a family, was slipping away. I could have done it. I could have married him that summer and been equal partners, prisoner and profiter of the whole shebang. I was forced to make a decision and when it all came down to it, I chose myself.

I chose not to get married and in doing so subconsciously chose to let the old Alex die. It wasn't overnight. But when I knew marriage wasn't the right answer, that vows and a party wouldn't make any of my current situation better, I was letting go. The proposal really took this already gut-wrenching scenario to a whole new level. All I had wanted for as long as I could remember was to get married. I wanted to be the wife, the mother, to have the household and do all the things young families do. But this wasn't right. It was so divinely clear that we were supposed to meet. It just wasn't clear why... until this moment. I knew I couldn't go through with the wedding. Heck, call me a gold digger until you learn that fact. I would have been financially set if I had married him. And it also would have likely been the biggest self-destructive decision I could have made. But I didn't. The pressure to just get married was so prominent, and mostly from my own mother. Talk about heartache. She was watching her daughter's life go up in smoke. She pushed so hard for a wedding. It's like everyone needed some illusion of a silver lining to carry them through. But I was done falling on swords.

Although I had reached this conclusion internally, I ended up throwing an engagement-meets-end-of-treatment party. I moved through this one like a zombie bride-to-be. It felt completely unreal to have our friends and family gather for such a façade of a celebration. It's important to acknowledge milestones in life and ending his treatment was certainly one to honor, but this party was more about appeasing my mother and quieting all the chirping about when we were going to get married. It's as if our reality was too heavy for even the people closest to us, so they had to shift the dialogue to asking about a wedding. Despite this party having "wedding" written all over it, I knew we were not getting married. So many of our friends and family thought we were going to surprise everyone that night by tying the knot. We didn't, although my look was quite bridal and the budget would have said otherwise. Instead of gifts, we asked for everyone to give us their favorite record. I couldn't bring myself to receive crystal and china and what may be considered normal wedding gifts. So records it was. My part of the collection now hangs on the main wall at Soul Dive Yoga.

In hindsight, I'm proud of myself for allowing my childhood bridal dreams to die, for releasing the fear of perception and judgment that I was abandoning my dying fiancé. That's all very real, and still is. But when it came down to it I had to choose myself. I was 33, I was not sick, and I had my whole life in front of me and maybe, just maybe, the reason why we met wasn't to see how far I'd go as the sacrificial lamb.

My decision had nothing to do with how much I loved him. This needs to be written here, for the record, loud and clear. Our love knew no bounds and transcends far beyond my earthly, human existence and ethereal realms. There is no one on this earth who will ever love me the way he did. What a gift to have received.

See, here's the thing about being at the bottom, or what I've coined as "landing in the shit." Being aware of it is just a small piece of the experience. When you're in it, whether day one or year two, you never know how long the transitional period is going to last. I am a hyper-aware and highly sensitive person with a first-hand view of mortality. Being in this shit sucked. Being in the shit alone, with no tools and no timeline, sucked even more. But here's the thing about awareness, even though I didn't know how long I would be there, I knew it wouldn't last forever. Even though I didn't know what exactly to do, I knew I had to do something. Even though I didn't know how, I knew I had to go through it. I had to sit in the middle of my very own dumpster fire, party of one.

The question I faced then was,

"Can you endure the burn to enjoy the bounty?"

I realized I could, and I did. The bounty might not have looked like I thought my life was going to look when I was living with the man that loved me more than life itself. And it certainly didn't look the way I thought it would when I was wearing the largest diamond I had ever seen on my left ring finger. But where I've landed is even more beautiful, full and wholehearted than I could have imagined on that day I knew everything was about to fall apart.

Sitting in the alley that afternoon with my hobbling dog and hidden tequila had a few perks. I met some people in the neighborhood I likely wouldn't have otherwise and had the opportunity to tell perfect strangers not to worry, their day was undoubtedly not nearly as tragic as mine. I made a promise to myself then: I would keep going. Whatever it takes, no matter how hard things get, you have to keep going. I knew, somewhere deep down, some larger purpose was going to reveal itself on the heels of getting tagged into a God-sized mission of taking care of my sick fiancé. Because the mission wasn't just about taking care of him. The mission was just as much about taking care of myself.

And that's what I did. I let it all burn to the ground. I let everything that defined my identity go so I could put the pieces back together and get to know Alexandra Marguerite Sabbag for who she was put on this earth to be. The process was my Soul Dive, of which this book is so aptly named after.

Chapter 5
Ugly Truths

Expectations hogtie our happiness to a certain outcome.

We have a unique ability as humans to repress traumatic experiences and erase unpleasant thoughts. We also have a mighty inability to release false identities and truths that repeat over and over in our internal dialogue. It seems the mental chatter never stops, especially when we need peace and quiet the most. In those moments we find ourselves haunted by our reality, searching for the way out, it seems the only thing we hear is noise. Negative self-talk is powerful and I'd venture to say one of the most impactful communication styles we've come to know as people. It's tragic, if you ask me. There is nothing healthy or helpful about the way we beat ourselves up inside our own minds. I don't know how we learned this behavior, but I know I'm not alone in attempting to minimize the destruction.

I give myself a lot of credit for having the awareness that I arrived at the bottom, or so I thought. There I was, holding only a glimmer of knowing this was pretty much as bad as it was going to get. But it hadn't gotten there yet. I was on the rollercoaster climb to the top, only the freefall was going to be more like a bottom out than a relief. It was like I was handed a sealed envelope of all the things that were going down in the flames, but I couldn't open it until it was time. Enter one of the many purgatory phases of my journey. In hindsight it was like being on a self-help scavenger hunt with a variety of breadcrumbs. Those I ate (in other words ignored), those that were toxic, (but I couldn't resist) and those that were lessons (of which I'd like to say I learned the first time, but alas, I am a 2x4 learner).

What's in the way *is* the way. The obstacles, the lessons and the divine redirects are the path. You don't have to keep searching for the trail, because it's right there. Nobody said you have to like it, but it's sitting directly in front of you. If you'd only have the courage to step forward. My path was in front of me too, I just needed to recognize it.

What I didn't quite understand, but I now know is true, is that I did decide—or at least my subconscious did—in that moment of acknowledging and accepting my life was falling apart, that I wanted to heal. I had no idea what I was signing up for. But the truth is we *choose* our path and I had chosen mine. I knew where I wanted to be and had absolutely no idea all the things I needed to do to get from awareness, Point A, to healed human, Point B. What I know now but didn't know at the time is there is no end to healing; it's a continual process; I was just unaware of the rules of engagement when I stepped into it.

I had signed up for it, but this concept of accepting the call without fully knowing what I'm saying yes to was totally unfamiliar to my then 3D human self. I didn't understand consciousness, had minimal familiarity with mindfulness and had no idea about nervous system regulation. But I signed on, and I know I did because my body moved in that direction. It was me and my mind that constantly held us up. My body knew what to do because I somehow got to the yoga mat almost everyday. Whether you can relate to my sorrow or your own, you know how hard it is to put one foot in front of the other and move your body. Thankfully, this had become second nature to me and is something I'll always be grateful for.

As much as I'd like to report that I surrendered my way into my whole self, I didn't. I have spent the better part of my life pushing the proverbial rock up the hill. I have always had a firm idea of how things should be or what they should look like. That's been my intention, my goals. The shoulds, obligations and expectations are how I lived my life up to this point. I didn't start fully thinking for myself until my mid thirties. Given I'm penning this at 38, that's not much time. (Hello self, nice to have you, pleased to meet you, grateful to continue knowing you.) Sometimes we hit points in our life where we get so disconnected to who we are we start from scratch. We get reintroduced to the soul in the human suit we put on in this thing called life. This was me: Dismembered, deconstructed and disconnected. But I was all zippered up into one human body. I cringe at the thought and it breaks my heart that so many people I meet are experiencing the same feelings. If we could only look at ourselves in the mirror with kindness, compassion and love. If only.

Growth doesn't happen overnight. Do you need to hear that again? No matter how much you drop in and devote all your might to moving through, it is a process. There is no plant medicine or shamanic journey that can take all your baggage up in smoke and spit you out a fully healed and evolved person. Trust me, I would have done that thing by now, wouldn't you? One big old mushroom journey for the win! In one way, out the other. We would pay so much money for that, but it's not how it works. The work is work for a reason. The work is arriving at the awareness that your life is out of balance and in dis-ease and then committing to shed the many layers required to realign with your purpose for a more peaceful life. There is no established timeclock for how long this takes. The truth is it takes as long as it takes. I hate this reality. I want things done yesterday so I can just "move on." I felt victimized by the totally unfamiliar process of healing. But I was still who I was before the diagnosis. A few months wasn't nearly enough to rewire my thoughts, establish new patterns of behavior and learn from my life experiences.

This is where the rubber meets the road and honestly, when my life started to get pretty darn ugly. There were so many truths that I needed to accept (most of which I wasn't ready for). I had only accepted one truth: my life was falling apart. But that was a bit too broad. I hadn't yet accepted that the life that I thought was being built was actually burning to the ground. I hadn't accepted that the man I loved the most, and who loved me back, wasn't going to be in my life. I hadn't accepted that my dreams of a family and a beautiful Lincoln Park Brownstone weren't happening. The list goes on, so much that the truths became almost impossible to accept and the climb to the other side was almost too much to bear. Imagine you're slowly ascending up a ladder. And with each rung you learn another truth, and another, and another. At some point the ladder is all the way up in the heavens and you can't wrap your mind around how you'll get to the top. It's like a game of a truthbomb whack-a-mole that never stops. The truth is there is no top, and this is the work.

It's pretty hard to do the work with no tools, eh? I didn't have them and even if I did, they would have been tucked high up on a shelf I couldn't reach. My ladder was occupied, coming to grips with the ugly reality that became my life. As I sank deeper and deeper down into the bowels of my own existence, my shadow side really took over. My patterns came flying to the surface in an effort to mask the devastation. The self-soothing and self sabotage arrived and I gave them both power. Today I'd invite the vices and the sabotage to the table, pull out their respective chairs and allow them to sit down. I can be with those demons now whereas then, they felt like friends and I allowed a hostile takeover of chasing men, over-drinking, emotional destruction and pure emptiness.

One of the hardest truths to accept? It gets worse before it gets better. And you have to let it. I thought the worst was the diagnosis and six months of caretaking. In hindsight, that was only the beginning. That was simply the event that struck the match. In the grand scheme of things, it was only the spark. The worst was coming. I wasn't prepared and it was dark. I hated the dark.

I remember the weekend he was plucked out of my life. The few days prior were the darkest of them all. I was way in over my head, trying to manage his mood swings, severe depression, anger, rage, substance abuse, and the fact that his body was failing in ways I couldn't physically manage. I phoned for help. His brother made it clear: Call if you need me and I'm on the next plane. I made the call. His mother arrived. I remember handing her my engagement ring, in pieces. A few days later she took him home. I was left alone, surrounded by remnants and rubble of what our life was together. I was left with more than the physical cleanup of cohabitation. My heart was shattered and my soul was in shambles.

Our home had become a toxic lair and I had nothing left in me to fix it. The six months leading up to this moment I didn't have—or rather I never took the space—to really feel or refill my own cup. This is one of the most harmful byproducts of fight or flight. We lose the ability to feel how things really are because we become obsessed with control. Physically, the sympathetic nervous system takes over, pumps out the adrenaline, and creates a façade that we can keep going. That was me. I was so consumed with my role as caretaker I lacked the capacity to get real with the self-destruction that was happening and take care of myself. Sound familiar?

I was no different, but there I was, left alone with no financial support, no job and no person. The bottom was falling out and as it did, I started to resist. I fully admit I did not step on the path to heal in July, and certainly didn't that October. Instead I put both feet on the high speed train of avoidance. I saw the ladder and it was way too high to climb out. I didn't want to hurt anymore and had enough heartbreak to last many lifetimes. So I tried to circumvent the entire call to go through. I ignored all the invitations to heal and just wanted this painful period to be over. I resorted back to wishing for what I had always wanted: my white knight of a man to enter the scene and save me from suffering. Surely a man would want to come in and make this all better. Men love saving women, right? I actually believed this would be the way out. No kidding.

I landed in a place that made it impossible for me to relate to anyone else. I struggled to maintain friendships. I didn't know what I needed, and if I did it seemed the list was too long I didn't know where to start. As a result, I pushed people away. My friends would try to support me, attempt to coax me out of the house. I was constantly struggling. From the moment he was diagnosed, I always felt guilt that I was going to be able to do things he wasn't. The guilt was followed by shame. I failed. Our relationship failed and I didn't save him. I beat myself up for years over the fact that I walked away from him. I developed an abandonment complex that still rears its ugly head in my life today. I not only abandoned my dying fiancé, but I abandoned myself. He abandoned me by getting sick and leaving. Everyone abandoned me. *Me me me.* I was a victim. I still have to be with this. The abandonment has shown up in business, and in my personal and romantic relationships. Healing is not an overnight job, my friends. It is one of my biggest demons and as much as I wish it would just go away, that's not how it works. In the final quarter of 2019, I finally made it all the way to rock bottom. I hit a physical and emotional breaking point. I was overcome with guilt, shame and failure wrapped in a giant blanket of sadness and heartbreak.

My old patterns flooded back over my life like toxic bandages delaying my process to finish falling apart so I could put it all back together. The biggest was my relationship with men. I deluded myself into thinking that someone was going to fall in love with me enough to save me from this devastation. I met someone the weekend he left. I decided that person would be my knight in shining armor. It was what I always did. So in hindsight, while I do carry embarrassment and shame about this, I'm not surprised.

My boy-crazy seeds were planted back in high school, really the first time in my life when boys actually paid attention to me. Remember, I wasn't pretty as an adolescent. I was overweight, had frizzy hair, and a lethal combination of glasses and braces. Luckily, I grew upward of seven inches one summer and matured out of this awkward phase. I didn't fully come into my looks until I went to college, and then overnight it was like this massive wave of freedom descended over me. I was finally pretty and had no curfew. Let the games begin!

The older I got, the more I craved male attention. It was like my kryptonite, fueling the validation I thought I needed from male strangers since my early twenties. I really never grew out of it, but as I got older and went through my healing journey I did double click on it quite a bit. It made me question whether I've had abuse or trauma with men. I started dabbling in spiritual healing modalities, which included doing plant medicine journeys and Akashic Record work, thinking that if I didn't have any male trauma in this lifetime maybe something would surface from my subconscious. I learned a valuable lesson: If you go digging for dirt your hands will get dirty. There was nothing there in the brief sweep and it felt like I was on a quest to create something out of nothing if I didn't stop. The practices took me into a false light and away from my faith.

Then I looked at DNA. My grandmother had five husbands, followed by boyfriends in the nursing home until the day she died. I took a deep dive into the concept that some kind of pattern can be passed down through women based on this claim: When your grandmother is pregnant with your mother, you are actually there, as an egg, in your mother, in your grandmother's womb. This theory would imply that I inherited my unhealthy pattern with men from my grandmother. My mom didn't, but apparently like all things DNA, it can skip a generation. Wonderful, thanks for the gift. It helped me to have someone to blame—to release fault. Since I wasn't ready to take responsibility for my own pattern, it felt good to source science as a way to put it on someone else. And since my grandmother died years ago, she can't really say one way or another. There. Buried under the rug.

The boy crazy pattern has been with me for decades and like most unhealthy patterns, they manifested other false truths that I hadn't addressed. If the guy loved me, I was lovable. You can ask my closest friends what my agenda was going out at night. Find men. Get a boyfriend. Become a wife. I feel sorry for my younger self. I didn't have enough respect and love for myself, I had to go fishing for it from some nobody in a bar. But alas, while I could sit here and pity the insecurities, some credit is owed to the ways in which this pattern brought some joy. Serial dating came with some serious perks: Spontaneous vacations, theater experiences, invitations and connections. I got to see so many parts of the world my budget wouldn't have allowed for. I went wine tasting in France and Italy, on a sailing trip to Croatia, and flew to Hawaii with 24 hours notice. What I might have lacked in self-respect for the better part of my adult life I more than made up for in passport stamps. Life can be too heavy not to count the small victories.

Looking back, my pattern with men is the most challenging part of who I became as an adult. What I wanted was a partner, my forever guy, a husband. But my behavior was not conducive to serious relationships, marriage, monogamy, or long-term partnership. I had quite literally made a part-time job out of dating. If my grandmother theory has any merit, this one is rooted in some kind of karmic cycle that skipped my mother and went straight to me. When my world fell apart, I fell back on my biggest weakness: men.

I spent eighteen years in Chicago dating every sports-obsessed bro that I could find. I had a series of fairly unfulfilling relationships that I fooled myself into thinking would go somewhere. I recognized my forever guy probably didn't live there, given our ideals likely wouldn't align (broad-sweeping statement for sure, but after almost two decades of coming up short, can you really blame me?). When I moved to California, dating was one of my only forms of social interaction so naturally, I gravitated to an app for some plans and at the very least, perhaps I would meet some new friends. Also, I used the excuses of, a girl's gotta eat, he has a sailboat, I could get a new client out of this, I need a date to a function, I'm the new girl in town and need some kind of social life. It was all lipstick on a pig. It still is. I fell back into this pattern time and time again, and the more I became aware of it, the more desperate I became to break it.

One of the biggest truths about healing is this: it's not linear. You can absolutely repair parts of your soul while others are still flourishing in the toxic nonsense. If we addressed all the darkness at once we'd experience some kind of spiritual shock. As time went on and I began seeing the light, my toxic traits with men were very much still present. And they even evolved a bit—how fun! Unhealthy pattern growth, I've got your case study right here. Before I met my fiancé I was chasing dreams and dating high caliber men. I have to admit, while I was still forcing marriage (something that failed each and every time), at least the ones I was spending my time with were upstanding individuals. In my early thirties, before my fiancé got cancer, my confidence, standards and self-respect were quite high.

Here's another hard truth: Trauma has a ripple effect that shatters more than just the central object in its path. It broke my soul into pieces, crushed my confidence, heightened my insecurities, fueled my anxiety, launched my abandonment complex and so much more. My trauma response is anger and coupled with the fight or flight that I slipped into, it properly wedged itself between my mind, body and soul. The trifecta of which makes me up was disconnected, yet shoved inside the body I was forced to operate everyday. I didn't realize how much repair and healing was required.

In hindsight, it's very clear what was happening. The fires were starting everywhere and the places I resisted letting go were just going to burn bigger, creating more rubble to sort through on the other side. But we can't see the other side when we're placed at the bottom of the ladder and told to climb. We just see the lift, feel the weight, and fight the invitation to put one foot in front of the other. We feel alone, isolated and unrelatable to the world around us. We retreat, act out and refuse to turn in and sit with the feelings of unknowing and discomfort: Mainly because we don't want to hurt anymore. We get heavier and heavier, picking up bag after bag of junk that isn't even ours to carry. When our trauma is too much to bear, we seek solace in others. The old misery loves company, so we start to pile on other people's stuff. It's a trauma bond, and it won't help you get through it; it will only delay your own process by further holding you back from your own healing journey ahead.

This is an awful place to be. I know because I've been there, and I also know because I've witnessed others standing at the base of the ladder. We can't do it alone, but so often we refuse help. I had offers for support. The entire time I took care of my fiancé, people were dropping off food, taking him on outings, helping with Alfie and more. But after he was gone, I had dipped into the darkness so deeply

I lacked the ability to really receive. It happens fast, you know. One minute you're all optimism and butterflies and the next you're sinking in quicksand. I pushed offers for help away and I fell hard into the victim mindset that no one understood. To be fair, no one *did.* But we can't judge someone's ability to empathize by lived experience alone.

Our shadow self loves a good victim moment. *Woe is me,* and doom and gloom are where victims thrive. You may think the world is happening *to* you and not *for* you. If you've been there, or know someone who lives perpetually in this state, then you know refusing support because the person offering "doesn't get it" is only harming your (or their) own healing. We're not giving people enough credit when we push them away. Humans are innately good and designed to support one another. We were meant to live in community, because we thrive as a pack. It's primal. The offer to help doesn't have to come from a place of "I know what you're going through." It needs to come from a place of love, compassion, kindness and empathy. We have to believe that. I know it's easier said than done, because I was so broken I couldn't mentally get there. So I pushed people away. I retreated and started building up all the walls that kept me isolated and safe. You don't have to go quietly into the night to let a part of you die. There are people around you who will hold your hand, and your hair back, as you release the past so you can make way for the future. No one said it had to be pretty and no one said you'd like it. But this is the truth: isolation doesn't fix it. Going into the cave with the goal to come out with a shiny bow on your head that screams "healed human" is not real.

If you take nothing from my experience, remember this: the healing journey doesn't require you to sit on the bench during the process. The healing journey is an interactive experience between your mind, body and soul and it requires movement. It requires life. We are wired for life, friends. So keep living, even while you're healing. Keep living so you keep moving. Keep moving so you keep growing. I didn't do that. I stepped out of my own life for about eighteen months until I felt like a caged animal and had to tap back in. Funny enough, just as I was coming off the bench, the world was going on lockdown with Covid. Oh timing and the practical jokes from God. It's like he looked at me and said,

"I told you not to stop, now you're really benched."

I call these periods of purgatory. Real 3D life purgatory. It's the waiting room, the liminal space, the space between where we came from and where we are going. I love talking about them and absolutely hate when I'm dropped in. But that's the ugly truth. Sometimes we're called to sit on the bench and wait; other times we're invited back into the ring for growth. Either way it's living, not retreating. It's community, not isolation. It's movement, not stagnation. And it's freaking hard to accept when we can't pry our cheek from our own self-pity pillow.

Chapter 6

Unhealthy Patterns &
Unimaginable Stories

Pretty girls get dumped too.

I designed my life so that I could someday wrap a beautiful bow around it. I wanted the perfect man, the published wedding and the picturesque home. The first company I founded at age twenty-five set me up to live this dream life of getting married, creating a family and thriving as an entrepreneur. I love how in theory everything you think is perfect is still so flawed—down to the fact that the reality I was trying to create was a complete and total departure from the independent, driven woman I was becoming. My living from a place of "should" began in my early twenties. I'm not a dreamer, this is just honestly what I thought I wanted and whatever the cost, it was going to be my reality.

A funny thing about this one (more jokes from God!) is that I did build a company that facilitated this exact dream. It just wasn't for me, it was for my Number Two. Ashley and I started working together in our late twenties when she was newly married and ready to start a family. Fast forward, two kids, two houses and that multitasking mom life later, she was doing the thing I thought I would be doing for myself. And I got to watch.

All I wanted to be was a wife. My parents never put pressure on me to settle down and get married. In fact, they never put pressure on me at all. As long as I was happy, they were happy. Failure was allowed in my house, it just personally wasn't an option for me. I was an okay student, received mostly A and B grades, and the occasional C showed up now and again in subjects I just didn't like (read: math and science). I remember getting so stressed as a kid about pressures. It was almost like I was absorbing the pressure my peers were feeling from their parents. Some of the best advice my mother gave me was around the ACT and SAT tests. She told me to put the papers down and go get ready. Shower, do my hair, put a little makeup on and feel good about how I was showing up. Then, as she reassured me I would go to college she said,

"*Someone* will take our money."

She was right, per usual. The only pressure my dad offered was perhaps I should take just one business class in college. I ignored it, and suffered countless frustrations as I embarked upon my own solo-preneur journey years later.

If I had to guess, I think it came from the fact that I was essentially an only child and most things I did were solo ventures: riding horses, playing the piano, entertaining myself with no siblings to play with. I have always craved companionship and at some early age defaulted to the fact that companionship had to be a husband. Try as I might to get there, I've failed each and every time. On a few occasions I've wished arranged marriages were a thing in our culture.

Let someone else find the man and negotiate the terms. I'll just show up in white and pray there's enough wine that I'll fall in love with him. I think my parents would do right by me. They'd find a Godly man, tall, handsome, gainfully employed (as in multiple homes and a private jet), ready to commit himself to a beautiful woman. What's so hard about that?

Side note, the closest I ever got to an arranged marriage was a set-up that came through Josephine, one of my best friends from college. She was at a wedding with her husband where she met a tall, handsome fella from Houston. She told him about me, showed him a picture and shared my phone number. He reached out and after a few unsuccessful attempts at meeting in one of our home cities, we took the show on the road and I joined him for a business trip in Vegas. Our first meeting was at Chicago's Midway Airport. We had a cocktail before boarding and started the get to know you process on the three hour journey west. While our story didn't end in wedded bliss, it goes down in my history books as one of the riskiest attempts to find love I've ever agreed to. Let the record show, I'm a yes woman when it comes to love, and this wasn't the craziest thing I agreed to in my quest to find it.

I had lived on my own since I was eighteen, and while I was growing into my independence, my decision-making was a pretty direct line from my parent's preferences. I'll say this for the record: none of it was bad, it just wasn't me. My mother could spend all day at Neiman Marcus. I was always conflicted. I didn't want to be there, but I absolutely loved the new outfit I got to wear out to dinner that night. It wasn't until my late twenties I realized how much I needed to move my body and enjoyed being outside. When my parents would visit I would tell my mom I'd meet her at the department stores later because I wanted to go to yoga and then walk down to Michigan Avenue. Her response was always,

"Why?"

I didn't have the words then, but I do now: Shopping just didn't and doesn't do it for me.

The living out of shoulds, societal expectations and parental opinions sneak up on you. I went out almost every night because I thought that's what I "should" be doing in my twenties. I drank excessively because that was the lifestyle in Chicago. I got dressed up all of the time because that's just what people did. Or so I thought. Apparently there's a whole other world over in California where people wear glorified pajamas to dinner; some of those people are even multi-millionaires. But I didn't have this information then. I got dressed up because that's what I thought I was supposed to wear to get men to pay attention to me. It's fronting, not communicating or connecting. What was actually happening was destructive to my health, wounding my nervous system every time I made a decision out of pressure or expectation. It was taking me further and further away from who I really am and my purpose. It was allowing these unhealthy patterns and belief systems to take over, perpetuating the cycle of acting out of pressure and obligation.

Looking back, my life looked quite enviable from the outside. International travel, great adventures, elevated dinners, handsome men. What's wrong with that? Easy answer, nothing. None of how I was living was bad, it just wasn't entirely me. Sure having these things can be gratifying. But it all started pretty small and over time slowly chipped away at my soul. I ended up drifting further and further away, allowing the pressure cooker of *shoulds* to heat up, silencing the internal feelings and intuition of what would be life-giving, infusing passion and purpose into my daily choices.

Had you asked me when I was twenty-five what my purpose was, my answer would have been to get married. If I'm really honest with myself, since as early as I can remember, every single time I left the house I was looking for my husband. My dating experience was for marriage; I never simply leaned into the pure joy of getting to know someone or enjoying the company of a man in an effort to learn more about myself. What's more, I also never learned how to properly vet a man to see if he was even eligible to earn the title of my husband. I had always been a chameleon of sorts. Who am I? More like, "Who do you want me to be?" I would cook my boyfriends extravagant meals, pack them lunch and do my best to show up as arm candy at the fundraiser or company dinner party. I even went so far as to cheer for sports teams and do the whole big game day ritual when in reality, I couldn't care less about sportsball. I was never in a long term relationship with anyone; in fact my longest relationship might have been twelve to eighteen months. The reasons were many, and I have to be okay with the fact that I just didn't meet "the one." But all that time serial dating, I wasn't 100% being myself. I was adapting to win the title of "Mrs." and it is no surprise that each one of these relationships went up in smoke.

My first boyfriend didn't come until college. He was awful. But nothing is for nothing. What he lacked in morals, values and overall kindness he made up for by being the catalyst to the best decision I ever made. A few weeks prior to my 21st birthday I decided I wanted a dog. My two best friends, Natalie and Josephine, were on the mission. We picked a day, Natalie's itinerary in hand, and hopped around the city to find the perfect match. Our first stop was at Collar and Leash in Chicago's Old Town neighborhood, and this was where I found him. He was the first one I held. Natalie encouraged us to press on, not to make any snap decisions. I obliged, but couldn't get this little Yorkie out of my mind. We went back to that first shop in Old Town at the end of the day where I plucked him out of a little girl's arms. Her father informed me she was only playing with him, and even so, I didn't care. He was naughty, an ankle biter and totally played hard to get. It was love at first sight.

I started negotiating the price with the shop and after a bit of back and forth, I freaked out and handed the little jet black feisty bundle back, leaving without him. I cried the entire night and went back to the shop early the next morning. I sat on the doorstep until they opened and immediately handed multiple forms of payment over so he could officially be mine. After the transactions I went to the 24-hour Starbucks and waited. In less than an hour I returned to find my new furbaby all fluffed up with a giant red bow around his neck. I took home this sweet baby boy just a couple weeks before my 21st birthday and it was the best decision I ever made.

I didn't tell my parents I got a dog. When it had come up in the past they threatened to cut me off. In hindsight, this is funny, we have always been dog people, but I heeded the warning up until this point. Alfie was maybe ten weeks old when my dad was in Chicago for a Cub's game with some of his guy friends from church. After the game we had plans to meet at Kelly's Pub, one of the best bars of all time and conveniently located a block from my apartment in Lincoln Park. As I was walking up I heard one of his friends ask my dad if I had gotten a dog. My dad quickly answered, "no." As I got closer I put the dog in my dad's arms and said, "This is Alfie Sabbag." His heart melted and within days a pink Juicy Couture dog bag arrived at our doorstep. It was over. Alfie was instantly a part of the family and as far as my mother was concerned, her first grandchild from me. Eight pounds of pure love and fury has ruled my heart (and my life) ever since. From college to Covid, caregiving and creating a beautiful life for us both, Alfie has been there. He's also had a front row seat to my love life… largely unimpressed, I wonder if anyone will ever win over his heart as they're trying to win over mine as well. We always have and always will be a packaged deal.

As far as my love life was concerned, I was a bit of a late bloomer in that department. I dabbled with chasing and being chased, but I was never really "going out" with someone until then. My post-college boyfriend was what I'd consider my first real relationship. I was about twenty-three, and he was a few years older. It was through him that I met my first group of post-college friends. And it was through them, and a love for day drinking on New Year's Day, that I met Tom. He asked how my year was going, and seeing as though we were only a few hours in, it was amazing. He was 6'6", blonde, from the east coast and worked in finance. *Check, check, check, check.* This was going to be the one. (He was not.) A year and some change into our relationship he knocked on my door and broke up with me out of the blue. Then he moved to Japan. Apparently I was so bad he had to move across the world to take some space.

I had never experienced heartbreak until this moment. There was no warning, no conversation, just done. Perhaps there were signs, a heads up of sorts, but I wasn't hearing it. I was stunned, stopped dead in my tracks. I consumed nothing but red wine and soy lattes for weeks. My mom came in to do her best to console me, to offer some distractions and damage control. My spirit was crushed and never really had the opportunity to repair. It was in this period I met an older man. I was blind to my surroundings, reeling in my own sorrows and trying to keep my first business afloat. I had started it just before Tom broke up with me. This older man asked if we could meet to talk about the nonprofit he ran that needed publicity. I agreed. It was networking. Who was I to say no to networking?

So we continued to "network." My delusional thought patterns couldn't recognize he wanted to date me. I eventually caved, not because I wanted to, but because I just wanted to be saved. The kicker with this one was that he was actually the guy that would have given me the life I thought I always wanted. I wouldn't have had to work, could have spent my days as I wished, and shown up as arm candy.

You know, some women are cut out for this. They can slide right into a man's life and enjoy it. At times I envy these women. If I'm honest, I still think this is what I'm looking for. But I was offered this life on a silver platter and resisted it so greatly. I was a young business owner and the thought of giving my business up gutted me. I learned what it's like to get jewelry after every fight, that I would get to go to Hawaii with twenty-four hours notice, and stay in the most lavish hotels around the world. On paper, this is what I wanted. In reality, I rebelled. I fought so hard to keep my independence that I would go out and not share where I was going. But here's the thing about men with money: if they want to know where you are they'll find out. He always knew. I was trailed, watched and then punished for it later. And I didn't leave. I would try, and when I did, some even more extravagant trip would show up in the future too near to let go. I am not a subtle learner, if you recall. And this boyfriend really made me pay the price. We went to Europe for ten or so days, basking in a blend of cities and wine tasting in the French and Italian countryside. Our first day in Paris he got the flu. So I did what any woman would do and enjoyed myself with his Amex while he was sick at the hotel. His flu was a quick hit and after a couple days we were en route to Bordeaux. The night we arrived we had massages and sat down for a beautiful traditional French dinner. Hours later, I was laid out on the bathroom floor, violently ill like I had never been in my life. I had received numerous pings that told me not to go on this trip. Apparently my intuition was working, I had just refused to listen. It certainly would have served me well at this moment!

Apparently I had Norovirus, which hadn't yet made its way to the US. For the next few days I grew in my appreciation for heated bathroom floors, couldn't keep anything down, and had multiple doctors visit me in the room with shots in the butt to quiet my nausea. Let the record show, while dying in a fancy hotel room is super bad PR for them, I would actually be quite fine with it. From what I've seen it sure beats the pants off your run of the mill hospice care.

The man I was with introduced me to the concept I later learned was emotional manipulation. While I was releasing my insides, he would apologize for ruining our trip to Europe, saying he was sorry I was having such a bad time. *Bad time?* I was practically dead on the bathroom floor. Anything would be an upgrade. I was desperate to go home, but even in this pre-Covid time, I was unfit for an airplane.

As the days went on, my windows for existing without vomiting were getting longer and longer, so we continued with some of the itinerary. I placed a call to my great aunt, in her 90's at the time and full blooded Italian. I asked her what to do for an upset stomach. She prescribed pomodoro and red wine, citing the acidity would settle my stomach. No argument here, and to this day, a classic bowl of pomodoro sauce over noodles does the trick every single time.

Once we were back stateside, I ended the relationship. To say it didn't go over well is an understatement. To not credit my mom for her advice not to go would be amiss. I said yes because I was immature, wanted to go see all the things and stay in all the places. Not because I loved this guy or thought we were going to be together. Lesson learned: If you ain't in it, don't get on the airplane. Unless you're exploring heated marble for a bathroom reno… but then, buyer beware, the stomach flu just hits different when you're in a foreign country.

I don't think any of my relationships have been for nothing. On one hand, I have to tell myself that to sleep at night. But on the other, when I really think about it, the lessons learned have been invaluable to my future self and future relationships. When I dated this older man I could have slipped right into his life and lived without a financial worry in the world. I could have shopped whenever I wanted, been treated to fine jewelry and never had to open a "Tuesday" bottle of wine. I had to go through this to learn one very valuable lesson: I'm not meant to be a trophy wife. Kept Woman isn't in my job description and I wasn't put here on this earth to live in someone else's shadow. I sometimes sit and wonder what life would have been like if I would have just said yes to it all. It's an easy story to romanticize, the truth nowhere to be found in the shiny details of not having to work. This calling works for some women and trust my honesty when I confess: I am sometimes jealous it's not for me. The grass can certainly be greener and with this one I'm blinded by the brightness. What a luxury to be the woman who leisurely has coffee, attends pilates or yoga, has lunch with some girlfriends and plenty of time to make (or make a reservation for) dinner. Clearly I didn't land in this position and on some of my hardest days, man I wish I would have.

The scars I walked away with after this relationship were pretty significant. I didn't have the emotional maturity to process the mind or mindset of the person I was with. I fought so hard for my independence in the partnership and failed to realize all I needed to do was step away from the stuff that came with him and *poof*, I had me back. I wasn't prepared to deal with big girl things like emotional control, getting trailed by a PI when I'd go out alone, intimacy issues, or his childhood abandonment issues. What I didn't know then is that anyone we enter into a relationship with—no matter how serious or casual it may be—we take on their stuff. I was consumed with galas and parties, building my business and living my best twenty-eight-year-old life. I had no idea how to navigate all that came with this one, and as a result, another failed relationship went up in flames.

The next guy I dated was as close to the one that got away as you could get. It was also my first introduction to the Peter Pan phenomenon I later discovered after moving to Southern California. I brought the emotional baggage of being controlled from my last relationship to the table and he brought his need for freedom, having moved to Chicago from New York where he lived with his last girlfriend. The only anecdote you need to know is this: We got into an argument on a road trip and when we stopped for gas, he put himself in the backseat. So I did what any grown woman would do and threw his headphones on the floor of the front seat so he was forced to talk to me. I told him I wanted to have children, not date one. We broke up (for the first time) after the trip.

But this one had potential. While there were some maturity gaps to close on both ends, we had a great run. He was the first boyfriend who said "I love you" and I said it back, meaning it everytime. He was joyful, thoughtful and taught me the art of ingredient hunting when making a certain dish. We would sometimes go to three to four grocery stores to shop. I remember how annoyed I was the first time he took me on the recipe treasure hunt. But after seeing his passion and how much love he poured into whatever he made, it stuck. To date, I will source the perfect ingredient no matter the distance or cost. He was a gem, and so was his family. Especially his mom. (Although she did make me dress up as Mrs. Claus on Christmas the year I visited.) My mom's response:

"This is what happens when you skip Christmas with your family."

Most of my adult life was living for someone else: the life plan my parents created for me, taking my mother's advice (which is sometimes excellent wisdom and other times totally insane nonsense). It all adds up, following social norms and just, more or less, existing among the masses. I was in my thirties and couldn't tell you what I wanted, what I was living for or how I wanted my life to unfold. The habits I was accumulating in my early adult years were manifesting into unhealthy patterns and addictions. Each relationship added another piece of emotional baggage to my shoulders, and each break up was soothed by another date, another glass of wine or a night out dancing with my girlfriends. I wasn't in my feelings, least of all in my body. I was making decisions based on other people's opinions; I didn't know how to intuitively feel my way through life (heck I couldn't even decide what to order for dinner most nights), and I made a part time job out of men so I could find a husband and all of my problems would go away.

I will say this. While most ended in tears and momentary tragedy, there was a lightness to my whole charade that is worth celebrating. I had it down to a science; I would challenge anyone to be more accomplished than I was at the dating game. See, in dating there are shapes. With the boom of online dating, no one was ever just seeing one person. The apps ignite "grass is greener" syndrome in nearly all users like none other. One guy must be better than the last. The basic shape of this pursuit is a triangle. I would have two front runners and then the default on the bottom (filed under "I'm lonely," "I don't want to be alone," "Maybe I'm missing something and I do actually like you," and many other justifications as to why we spend time with people we don't actually have feelings for). Then there might be a trapezoid, one front runner, two vying for the top and of course, the default on the bottom. The constructions of the shapes were a team effort. This is back when my PR company was in full motion. I would show up to work, Ashley and I would debrief a live dating diary over coffee, print off the profiles of men that were in the running, and construct the shape together. At times even the interns joined the fun. And while it was fun, entertaining, lighthearted and from an outsider perspective might have looked like I was living the young, single and fabulous life dream, it was exhausting and unbeknownst to me, depleting my soul. To sum it up: it wasn't what I wanted. Deep down I wanted my forever person.

While I can admit my achilles heel here, I will say this. I firmly believe in the opportunity to love and be loved while healing even the deepest and darkest parts of ourselves. My choices and experiences have definitely left a mark. I live with an anxious attachment style and have developed an abandonment complex. Even with my flaws, whether you want to call it looking on the bright side or totally delusional, I have forever been the romantic optimist and I know I'll find him, or he'll find me, or we'll drop into the vibration of our meet-cute destiny that is beautifully scrolled amongst the stars. Just please God, don't make it some short, chubby, random one-off online date. I'm looking for a handsome, wealthy, adonis of a man and I need a good story behind it.

While the unhealthy pattern with men has been, (and despite much awareness and intentional healing) might always be my biggest weakness, I've had some wild experiences that wouldn't have been possible without it. I'm happy to report that I've grown out of the toxicity and into gratitude. I'm a little miffed that my reality show "Married or Murdered" never made it off the ground; I had some seriously great content for that one. If you're like me, and you've lived through the revolving door of dating and run-your-legs-off in the hamster wheel of toxic masculinity, you and I both deserve a medal. So here's your slow clap, I see you. And because I believe there is a divine reason we go through our respective patterns, learn from our weaknesses and grow with each lesson, I've decided to spill the tea. This pattern sparked reckless choices, questionable decision making and loads of heartbreak. But I made it to the other side, and hand extended, I'm asking you to live vicariously through me for a little bit.

In my early thirties I traveled to Europe for three consecutive summers with my best friend from college, Natalie. It all started with a trip to Greece for my thirtieth birthday, the vacation we planned to kick off an annual travel series together. A few months prior to the trip I initiated a call to let her know I broke my foot. She responded that she was pregnant. The deal was off. Not a chance I was going to Greece with my pregnant friend throwing up off the side of our day party boat, sipping water at the club and hauling her belly around the beach. Nope, hard pass. So I pivoted, flew to Milan and spent a month with my Italian boyfriend traveling down the coast, meeting his family and showing my parents the Amalfi Coast with my local tour guide.

The next year didn't work for our trip either, so we reconvened with the globetrotting adventure for my thirty-second birthday: A trip to Spain. We began in Barcelona, went up to San Sebastián and I planned to end in Marbella with my parents. Flying into Barcelona from Chicago is quite possibly my favorite European flight. I would depart at 10:00 p.m., 500-mile upgrades placed, some wine, a little sleep and would arrive in Barcelona at 2:30 p.m. We were in the Soho House pool with a pitcher of sangria by 3:00 p.m. On this particular trip, we met a group right away: a blend of global citizens boasting gorgeous accents. Amongst the group was an amazing American woman who I still consider one of my sweetest soul sisters today, an Argentinian gal, and one of the most beautiful men I have ever seen, an Australian named Jim. I had fallen down the rabbit hole of hunk heaven. Foreign (check), hot (check), single (check). We exchanged numbers and made some loose future plans.

As Natalie and I were stepping on the elevator for an evening on the town, two American men got in after us. By the time we hit the ground floor we were invited to join a bachelor party later that night. We hadn't been in Spain for twelve hours yet and my ego was swelling by the masculine energy swirling around us. We ate tomato bread, polished off some Spanish red wine and joined the bachelor party until the wee hours of the night. We were treated like queens, had bodyguard escorts to the restroom and wanted for nothing on the champagne list. One of the handsome strangers, we'll call him Paul, was in his early thirties, lived in Manhattan, and wanted to see me again. We made some plans together once back in the states.

But for now, I was focused on more foreign affairs and our second night in Spain brings us back to Jim. The connection was fire. While Natalie and I were only in Barcelona for a few days, Jim and I made plans to go to Ibiza for a week at the end of my trip. I changed my flight, we found a hotel on the quiet side of the island and were essentially two strangers on a Spanish honeymoon together. We took a day trip to Formentera and ended the evening at a David Guetta concert. We did beach clubs and romantic walks, drank wine and talked endlessly about anything. I was already planning our life together and he was likely just tipsy philosophizing.

I fell so hard for this man I balled my eyes out the entire way home. The flight attendant actually tried to console me, asking what was wrong. All I could do was show her our picture. He was beautiful. I saw myself as beautiful in the photo next to him, tricking myself into thinking this was going to be the man I would marry. Let's be honest: he gave me absolutely no indication he wanted anything serious, was interested in marriage, would consider a woman from the states or would even think about visiting me in the US. We had a wonderful time, that was real. But the expectations I placed over the situation were my wildest dreams and quite the departure from reality.

I took an enormous risk, vacationing with a stranger. To say the least, I lacked any and all understanding that in doing so, I would develop a deep attachment to that person. None of that crossed my mind. I started fantasizing about moving over to Europe before we even stepped into our romantic time capsule together. Sure, I was in the moment, but totally carried away by what it could deliver. I carried my broken heart home to Chicago. Thankfully it was June, primetime in the windy city.

And then there was *the other one.* I went to see Paul in New York, and later he came to Chicago. Not surprisingly, it didn't go anywhere. But life has a funny way of preparing you for what's to come. That summer was filled with endless possibilities for love, and with each one I was given the opportunity to learn, approach things differently, or even not approach things at all (something I never even considered). I was continuing my part-time work of creating something out of nothing and thus, the pattern continued. That's the thing with patterns, even the ones that don't sound like much. If left unattended they start to chip away at you more. It wasn't just my heart that was getting hurt time and time again, my body was starting to take a beating as well. By the time September rolled around, I began experiencing some health issues. My nervous system was under attack and my symptoms were severe nerve pain. It was difficult to walk or stand for long periods of time and live the active lifestyle I was used to.

On Saturday, September 9, 2017, I was invited to join a group of friends at the Lincoln Square OktoberFest. I don't drink beer, but I had no shame in bringing my own bottle of wine. My girlfriend and I went, enjoyed some German fare and met up with the group that invited us. It was there, standing in a circle connecting with new people that I met my fiancé. My world stopped, my blinders went on, and I fell so hard and fast for this man I couldn't see straight. There is no stopping fate when it rolls by. That was us, fated to meet and fated to live through the experience we did together.

We connected on a soul level that day. At first blush he wasn't my type, but I didn't notice. He stood about 5'9", had shaggy hair, casual dress and wore a death metal band T-shirt. I saw none of that. I noticed his smile and the way he did anything he could to sit by me and get my attention. Four of us had dinner at Gather in Lincoln Square. We bantered as if we'd known each other for years, decades or lifetimes. We had the waiter convinced we had four kids at home. Our two other friends that joined us watched our connection unfold in real time. And later, they witnessed the painstaking heartbreak of unraveling. But that first night, we ended up on my roof deck until two or three in the morning. I wouldn't let him stay, and he didn't want to leave. He called me the next day and we spent every single day together from that moment on.

The historical catalog of my relationships all laddered up to the moment we met. Our souls aligned, as if they recognized each other and the destiny that was about to unfold. The last decade of my life did absolutely nothing to prepare me. All the baggage, heartbreak and toxic relationship experiences still fixed to my shaky shoulders as I stepped forward into this one. To be fair, his bags were pretty darn heavy as well. Despite it all, our love developed fast, and left little to no space for healing or dealing properly with our past. We just hopped on the high speed train and never looked back. We were dating for maybe two weeks when he asked me, in the back of an Uber, what kind of diamonds I liked. I was stunned. I had no idea what the diamond shapes were called so I kept saying I didn't know. He pulled out his phone, showing me a picture of all the names and shapes, surprised I had no idea. The only answer I could come up with was this:

"Big ones. I like big diamonds."

Chapter 7
Permission to Be

Through the lack of perfection and indisputable need for healing, you have permission to be just as you are, in this moment, the next, and the one after that.

I lived most of my thirties for someone else, and I'm telling you what I wish I knew then: You have permission to simply be as you are. You have permission to show up as *you* because you are enough. You have permission to be loved. Let's say that one again: You have permission to be loved. You are loveable. You are worthy of love. Nothing is wrong with you, nothing! We all need to heal. Through the lack of perfection and indisputable need for healing, you have permission to be just as you are, in this moment, the next and the one after that. It is your right to be you. You know what's funny? This is all fact without the permission part. It's just that somehow through being alive, the wires get crossed and we forget who we are. For me, the permission was required to start seeing myself as enough.

Had this been told to me in my early thirties I would have brushed it off and said,

"No kidding. I am me, this is who I am."

My words would have been loaded with defensiveness and insecurity. Because not only did I not know who I was, I had no idea how I was showing up. My mind and body were detached, having two completely different dialogues day by day. What I thought I should be doing and what I (the self) actually wanted to do were not the same. And I didn't listen to me, I listened to the influence.

Practicing yoga was a catalyst for meeting myself in a different light. What started as a purely physical way to maintain my physique morphed into a soulful deepdive. The practice became my lifeline and feels like it just began when things fell apart. The day after we were discharged from the hospital following my fiancé's diagnosis I went to the yoga studio. When I walked in, the teacher, who had a powerful anatomy-focused vinyasa voice, immediately saw my engagement ring and went nuts over it. I burst into tears. She was confused. I told her he was dying, relived the last four days since returning from Spain and it was in that moment my life changed. She didn't hug me, pity me, or offer her sympathy. She gave me permission. She told me the studio was my home, I was always welcome and I could simply show up exactly how I was. Whether I laid down on the mat and slept, balled my eyes out or pounded my frustration away, it was all available. I could simply be. This permission shifted my mindset. I found a place where I could go and show up in any way, shape or form. However I was, it was good enough. The fact that a space like this existed was new information to me.

So I showed up. I practiced almost every day. I had no power. I could barely get out of bed, least of all move myself through the class. My body was holding on to the trauma, reducing my mobility and flexibility as I entered into this time of panic, grief and sadness. I didn't make the connection, but my physical body was showing the world what was happening in my life. I was closed, achy, and weak just to name a few. I didn't have the understanding to honor where I was, but I kept showing up because I was given permission. It was during this time the practice shifted. Yoga's higher power struck and the practice became my lifeline.

I didn't know what was happening, really. My life was blurry, cluttered by the mixed emotions of caretaking and lack of taking care of myself. But in the midst of it all, my mat became my own little sanctuary in the studio that became my new home away from home. It sparked some curiosity. How can yoga, something I only knew to be a mostly physical experience, have such a profound impact on my life? I had heard about the spiritual side of the practice, but that hadn't made its way onto my mat quite yet, or so I thought. The curiosity prompted me to look into teacher training. One conversation later, I was enrolled and it started just after the first of the year.

I pursued teacher training to seek greater understanding of why and how yoga works. Surely there was some ancient secret sauce here and I wanted to get to the bottom of it. I had no desire to teach. I was at a point where I realized I had to do something for myself, to rediscover who I am and what I'm doing here. As I sat with the investment of the training I also considered a few other options. I thought about going back to French school to brush up on my foreign language, or taking up Second City classes to become fluent in stand-up comedy, or pursuing my sommelier certification to bring forward my passion for wine. Each one offered incredible learnings, but all of those involved drinking copious amounts of alcohol, which didn't feel like the right call for where I was at the time. Yoga teacher training won out, and I went straight into the deep after committing.

I am constantly amazed at how life prepares us for what's next. I embarked upon teacher training with the simple curiosity to learn, and little did I know I would be the owner of a studio in Southern California—preparing a space for anyone who walks through the door to come as they are, take what they need and simply be. There aren't enough places in the world where we can go, just as is. There are expectations, dress codes and social norms—all of which are our obligation to understand and meet. But yoga is different. I didn't know it at the time, but one little yoga mat holds boundless energy for curiosity, discovery, healing and expression. What started as a way to begin putting the pieces of my soul back together was planting seeds for personal growth, and the opportunity to give back in a way that offered me so much solace. In short, this is why Soul Dive Yoga exists in the first place.

To simply be is a gift. Do you know you have it? It's your birthright to be who you are. You don't need my permission and you certainly don't need anyone else's. Who you are is exactly why you're here. You knew it at one point, but it got lost in the shuffle of you trying to be who you thought everyone wanted you to be. We've overcomplicated it, really. It's far more simple to be who we are—heck, we own the manual. But we forgot. We lost the instructions and are trying desperately to get back to that place. A place of peace, equanimity and balance where we know wholeheartedly we are enough. The older we get the further we stray, and the more fear, doubt, worry, envy and lack make their way into our minds. Those things weren't there from the start; they somehow hopped on the bandwagon as we got older. This is another gift of aging: we get more and more delusional.

But the practice of yoga, this ancient science, allows us to come as we are and work through the emotions, thought patterns and complications we've brought into our lives. Yoga allowed me to let go. What is clear to me now is this: I needed to run away from home. But I only had an hour. Yoga seemed to be the only existing thing in my life that fit the timeclock.

My fiancé needed constant care. He had lost fifty percent field of vision, his balance was challenged and the exhaustion from all the treatment was debilitating. I hate how much he needed me. His independence was stripped away from him and the help handed over to me, his new girlfriend-turned-fiancé after only nine months of dating. To need this much care at that young of an age was unfair. It never occurred to me that he might have needed an out, an escape or just departure from his own reality in the way I needed it for me. I was too far gone in my own fear, despair and heartbreak to think he might have needed that for himself too.

Each day we came home from his daily radiation, I would tuck him into bed, get him settled with a guided meditation (Jack Kornfield was a go-to) and then I would go to yoga. He would sleep so soundly for two to three hours I knew I had enough time to get there and back home before he woke up. Alfie would snuggle right up into the bed and I could run away from that dark reality for a brief reprieve. I went daily, slowly letting yoga sink deeper into my tissues.

The deeper I dove into the practice the more it supported me back. After I went through teacher training I started to feel inspired, like I had a bigger purpose on this earth. I felt like I was a part of something, a chosen family of sorts. Yoga was a community that I could rely on, that was there to hold space and lift me up if I needed a little extra love. And I was grateful to give back. Teaching brought me so much joy. I can't remember a time in my life where I was more excited to show up for something than I was in those early days of leading yoga classes. I even flew across the country to teach two classes over the New Year. The music, students and opportunity to use my voice all inspired me. I couldn't get enough.

I was a couple months into teaching when I started to lose interest in my first business, AM Consulting. I had felt the calling to start my own business following five years at a PR agency. I wanted to be my own boss, craving freedom and autonomy. I had grown tired of serving corporate brands and felt my heart calling for fulfillment, the opportunity to work with missions that matter. I had started my boutique communications firm in 2010 that did fundraising and public relations for mostly non profits. Authenticity is at the center of who I am. (I also don't possess the skills to fake it.) The more I loved and believed in who I was working for, the better the results. Thus my criteria for sourcing clients: Do I like you? And no assholes.

I knew at an early age I wasn't meant to work for anyone else. (Although later in my career I did dip my toe back in those waters.) I was twenty-five, left my agency job and accepted $1,000 per month to support a highly regarded breast cancer organization. This didn't even cover my rent. The next month, I not only doubled my first retainer but added a second client, an organization that supported women's and infants' health, to my roster at the same amount. The business grew from there, out of love, devotion and a heck of a lot of sweat equity.

My identity was consumed by my business. I didn't exist separately from my career; my entrepreneurial spirit was the only spirit I knew and it was directly connected to who I was at my core. Seemingly normal, I think many entrepreneurs go through this and most working professionals fall victim to being identified by their work. I was eager for recognition and respect and this was my rite of passage to earn it. So I dovetailed my persona to my profession and slowly let me fall by the wayside.

I was entering my tenth year in business in the fall of 2019. After two offices, growing to a staff of seven at our largest, and supporting numerous philanthropic missions across the Chicagoland area, I was ready for something else, a change. I had no idea what, but I knew I needed space for this next venture to come into my life. I had flirted with leaving Chicago many times over the years. Each time the urge came up something would suck me back in. Whether it was a new client or another relationship, it was easier to choose to stay. Eighteen years is a long time and it's quite a bit to unravel. This time was different. I felt something coming and knew I didn't have the bandwidth to answer the bell with my current business obligations. One by one, I started ending contracts with current clients. To make up for some of the extra income, I taught as many yoga classes as possible at the studio. The difference: yoga filled me up where my business sucked me dry.

With each client contract I served I felt an even bigger sense of freedom. I felt empowered, like I was doing something for myself not in response to someone else. For as long as I can remember, the idea of closing that business felt like failure. Like I couldn't cut it because I didn't sell and take a seven figure exit. But let's remember why the company was founded in the first place. I wanted freedom, autonomy, and to build a family. All of these were achieved by someone in senior leadership, it just wasn't me. The fact that Ashley was able to have two beautiful children during her time working for AM Consulting is worth honoring and celebrating. Freedom might actually be harder to achieve than scaling up for the seven figure sale. I don't know for sure, but I can tell you striking the balance of freedom and bringing in enough income to enjoy your freedom isn't easy! That all said, there came a point where the work wasn't fulfilling. Waking up everyday to be in the role was daunting, annoying and became soul-crushing. It took me a while to arrive at this conclusion: I didn't have to keep my business just because I started it. It was okay to want something else, to want more and crave a new challenge. Choosing to grow and expand is not failure. Not only was the business successful, it provided the opportunity to mentor a number of bright young women and support their continued success. I was choosing to surrender into the nudge that Chicago might not be it forever and evolving my work as a professional was one of the most pivotal moments in my life.

I have always been brave when it comes to business. Man! I got more than I bargained for. It was the fall of 2019 when my teaching career really started to light up. It seemed like every day another teacher was sick. One by one they all started dropping like flies! Fast forward to March of 2020 and we were shut down, put into isolation and Covid-19 was a global pandemic. Covid pretty much launched my teaching career. I went from almost daily classes in the studio to teaching classes for the community online. It was fun at first, being able to flow alongside the students while I was teaching. And from home during a Chicago winter, another bonus!

The feelings I had around closing my business and the desire for a new challenge are best described as subtle nudges. It was when I felt the invitation to get ready, without knowing what was coming next. If I had to define it, I would say it was my intuition at its finest. I had started to become familiar with that "gut feeling" and was actively working on building the trust to lean in and listen. I remember in late 2019, when I felt like a change was coming, that I wanted more. I remember the awareness that I didn't have the capacity to answer the bell. Something in me sparked the need for space. *Create space for what's coming, create space so you can be ready.* So I did. One of my dearest friends (now a famed celebrity stylist in LA) came over and did a huge purge on my closet. She gathered over twenty trash bags of clothes, accessories, shoes, bags, you name it. I was ready to let go. This seems so simple and you might even say unrelated to what I was going through. But it's not. Our stuff holds weight, useless energy that keeps us stuck. And I was definitely stuck. I'd spent eight years in the same house accumulating thing after thing, outfit after outfit, with no letting go. That would make anyone stuck. It wasn't just my stuff, it was my fiancé's as well. The weight of our situation was still looming throughout the rooms of my beautiful once-sacred home in Chicago's West Loop.

The onset of the pandemic marked the official end of AM Consulting and the beginning of my work in the startup world. I got connected to a company based in Southern California that was a great fit with my marketing and healthcare experience through AM

Consulting. I was brought on as the Communications Director and two weeks later, told I needed to relocate to Southern California so I could work in person with the team. Within a month of relocating I became the Chief Marketing Officer and in mid-August, just shy of three months with the company, my email was turned off.

Nothing could have prepared me for this experience. My very first day in the office the CEO started making remarks about my appearance. As the weeks went by he would take me out for three to four hour lunches, refusing to let me go back to the office. He would insist we meet outside of the office, over wine and in private. He even showed up outside of my house. He cornered me and made sexual advances. He used his power as an attempt to manipulate me. When I rejected him, he hung my job over my head attempting to get me to submit to his advances.

I tried to handle the situation on my own, which failed. After I brought it to HR, who was also his assistant, my email was turned off. I have a federally filed sexual harassment lawsuit in the state of California. It has been three years since my complaint was filed with the EEOC. Not only has there been no justice, but the process has moved so painfully slowly there has yet to be a trial or court date set. To say that the system is a royal failure would be a dramatic understatement. The system is designed to protect corporate leadership, not advocate for women who have been victims to sexual harassment. As one lawyer brazenly asked me,

"Well were you raped?"

I said no. He went on to say it wasn't worth his time if I wasn't. Let that one sink in.

In August of 2020, three months after I had relocated to California, I had to get honest about where I felt called to be. California still felt like it was the place, and Chicago felt like I would be living in the past if I returned. So I started to let go. I tapped back into the feeling that there was more for me. Bigger challenges, more purposeful work. I took what I learned from purging my closet and applied it to my entire home. I started letting go of every physical thing I could. I put my house on the market and the first woman who walked into it, bought it. I returned to the Windy City for a six-week farewell tour. I let go of 90% of my belongings and officially moved out of my home on October 25, 2020. Ten years to the day after founding my first business.

I had been ready for a change for quite some time. I didn't ask to be sexually harassed by the CEO of the company that moved me to California, but accepting the position got me out of my complacent comfort zone of Chicago and for that reason alone I'm grateful for the experience. I was ready for a change of scenery, an upgraded lifestyle as I called it at the time. California had the DNA of what I was looking for. There was better weather for more time outdoors and access to the activities that filled me up—hiking in the mountains, long walks on the beach, incredible yoga and a whole bunch of strangers that had no idea who I was or what I had been through. It was a fresh start. But all of that newness was made possible because I allowed an old piece of me to die. I let go of the business that defined my identity, my relationships, friendships and the community that was so dear to me. I let go of the familiarity, my home, and a city that brought me into adulthood. I let go of the house that held me and my fiancé through tragedy, all of my furniture, style and the way of life I knew as a woman. I shed more layers in the process of listening to my intuition and following the nudge west than I could have imagined. I let go of every piece I had so tightly gripped in my fingertips as I said goodbye to the city, the people, the industries and the routines that I shared with Chicago for eighteen years. Through deep surrender, I allowed the western winds to blow me to the California coast.

Chapter 8
The Burn

If you find parts of your life on fire,
quit trying to fix it and fan the flame.

Can you endure the burn to enjoy the bounty? The answer is yes. I did, and you can too. The morning of my 33rd birthday, sitting in the waiting room for my fiancé's impending diagnosis, ignited the biggest fire I will ever have to endure in my lifetime. That day my entire life as I knew it started to burn to the ground. The fire kindled slowly, bit by bit. . . the unraveling of everything I knew. My relationships with my friends, family and business all began to burn. Everything I was attached to and defined by—my work, club memberships, network and party invites—were all slowly plucked from the grip of my palm.

We begin to learn the lessons of nonattachment from an early age. Kids build resilience through changing schools, friendships, hobbies, cities and for some, even countries. Children are champions of letting go, starting over and flowing through life. However, the older we get, the more we resist letting go. It's like our scarcity complex kicks into high gear when we take ownership and responsibility for our futures. We start to create the lives we think we want to live and when something doesn't go according to plan, we lose it, unable to cope and flow forward.

I didn't know it at the time, that my life as I knew it was burning down. If I knew it I'd probably have tried to throw buckets of water on it to stop the flames. I don't think I would have had the courage to willingly let it all go up in smoke. If I did, my guess is it all would have happened much faster. I feel like my life back then was running in slow motion, all the gripping, resisting and attaching delaying the inevitable until it was too late. It seemed one thing after another started to fall apart from that day forward. In hindsight, I know it deep down in my soul to be true. My life was set on fire and I had the *privilege* to watch it burn.

It didn't all go down at once. It was a slow burn and when something big would fade away, sometimes a little seed of something new would take its place. Fires are not all bad, you know. And they don't necessarily happen in one massive explosion. This one was a steady burn, traveling in multiple directions, leaving only remnants of what was once there and plenty of lingering embers in its wake.

The first thing to go was my dream of being married with children by a certain age. The diagnosis didn't just take away my person. That actually wasn't the thing. It took away the future I so desperately wanted. The diagnosis took a piece of me that was an identity I longed to be connected to: Wife, first and foremost. Mother, a distant second. I watched my future go up in flames when he got sick. While it was devastating to witness his slowly declining health and all the challenges that came with his diagnosis, it was worse watching my own future die. And not just die, but die slowly. This wasn't your average breakup where you take a four to eight week dating cleanse and get back out there. This was an unthreading of a lifetime promise, big soul-connected love, loss and the tender practice of letting go. I wish it went down as poetic as I make it sound but it didn't.

The end was ugly. We were both hurting in ways the other couldn't understand. There is a large part of me that thinks he let it get as ugly as it did so I would walk away. He wanted to spare me because he knew the outcome. Not because he immediately put one foot in the grave, but he had enough mindbody connection and was intuitive in ways most could only imagine, he knew what he was up against and he loved me enough to spare me the greater pain I would inevitably experience by sticking around. As gut-wrenching as that sounds, I remember him saying in the early days after the diagnosis,

"If you're going to leave, leave now. Don't wait."

I ignored it because at my core I fight; I do not flee. So he pushed me out. I don't think I would have the love or the bravery to spare my person in this way.

I did walk away, and in doing so, experienced numerous deaths in the wake of my decision. It was the death of my relationship, the death of my future life and dreams of being married, and of my role as a founder and business owner. I stepped away from AM Consulting when I started taking care of him because I didn't have the bandwidth for both. I handed my first baby, the company that identified me, over to my twenty-year-old intern and wished her luck. This one was a slow burn for sure.

My work has always defined who I was. Unraveling myself from AM Consulting, stepping away from the PR industry, from galas and fundraisers, the glitz, glamor and all the press was a fulfilling release. As I made more space, I welcomed my new passion for yoga. Teaching filled me up. It felt spacious, far less stressful and sprinkles of joy came back into my work that had left the building after so many years. Letting go of this world was necessary to make room for my purpose. It just took a few years to iron out.

As time went on I noticed my relationships changing. I was outgrowing friendships that I had had for years. Some friendships were grounded in shared history, others out of geographical convenience. But it was beginning to become clear we had less and less in common. Conversations became less frequent, get-togethers more sparse. As Covid tucked the world in, I leaned further toward recluse. So much of my life was out on the town, in connection, social and quite frankly energy depleting. When I was told I had to stay home, I was in full blown hallelujah amen from the choir mode!

After I moved, I comfortably settled into my California nook and quietly started over. One by one my friendships started dissipating. I was on a different path. My priorities shifted. After my engagement went up in smoke I spent a really long time feeling sorry for myself. I struggled to be happy for other people and it seemed at this precise time, many people I knew and had friendships with were getting married. I missed every single one of their weddings. I couldn't go. In some cases I would RSVP yes and bail at the last minute and in others, just say no because I knew I couldn't handle it. I wasn't emotionally healed to the point where I could show up and celebrate someone else. As hard as that is to admit and as embarrassed as I have been, that's the truth. This burn took out my future, my relationships, my work, my home, my community, and my friendships. Like all good burns, it took layers of who I am off of my proverbial body.

I was stripped down to the core, shedding fronts, posturing, fakeness, and false identities. I was burning through the many layers that had come on board my soul over the years and that had gotten me to an inauthentic version of myself. As they started to shed, a vulnerability laced with a bit of insecurity started to come over me. I was being exposed. I didn't have the security blankets that I so often covered up with—from the familiarity of a city to the casual acceptance of a drinks date because I didn't want to stay home alone. The raw reveal that comes with peeling back the curtain was staring me in the face saying,

"Okay, this is me."

I would be lying if I said it was easy to look at myself in the mirror with grace and love. As the burn continued, it was getting more personal and hitting closer to home.

It was becoming clear that I had developed an unhealthy relationship with men. The masculine side of who I was was critically wounded. I was attracting men that were unavailable because I myself was subconsciously going through such a massive shift, I couldn't possibly be available either. Even though I thought I was so readily available and willing to give anyone a chance, I wasn't. I didn't love, respect or honor myself either. Cue attracting men that are less-than, unworthy, and not loyal. How could I expect more when I wasn't capable of giving that level of treatment to myself first?

I went through two unhealthy relationships after my fiancé, both lasting less than six months and both ending in flames. While they looked nothing like each other, they were largely the same. I was never their priority, they weren't loyal and both were a complete embodiment of a Peter Pan. Both presented me an opportunity to either put myself on a pedestal and walk away because I wasn't treated the way I deserved or to try to change them. I did the latter, failing to learn in both relationships. I thought I could be the woman who made them settle down; I thought that one day they'd walk in the door and realize what a prize I was. Instead, neither did this. And it wasn't their fault. They were never going to, nor did either of them give me any actual indication they would. It is not someone else's responsibility to uphold your boundary. I didn't love and respect myself enough to demand better attention, nor did I have the guts to walk away when it wasn't delivered. Rest assured, I know better now.

It's hard to believe what I put up with. What has become clear is that in all the shedding, the layers and layers that I was releasing, I kept reaching for my final security blanket: men. It was the last ditch effort to make the burning stop. To go back to some familiar old pattern and expect it to be different. I did it twice, back to back. When the second relationship ended, it was just after the first of the year and I had landed on my word. The word was *surrender*.

There were many other things I needed to do. First and foremost, I needed to get to know myself and even bigger, fall in love with myself. That was going to take a little time. But what I needed to do to get there was surrender. I needed to let go, to allow my life to unfold. I needed to allow whatever else was seeing its way out of my orbit to go, and not to stop it. Including men. I needed to stop chasing empty love just for the sake of having it there. Those relationships were never going to be fulfilling and they were certainly never going to lead to the end game of getting married and having a family. So I surrendered.

Saying you're ready to let go and actually doing it are two completely different things. We can be aware, but without a practice, we lack the tools to execute. I knew the concept of non-attachment, releasing the grip and letting things go. I was taught. I understood. But I didn't have the practice to lean on during the summer when he was diagnosed. Surrendering takes discipline and a lot of grit to heal your mindset. Letting go, releasing, and surrendering is a beautiful place when we get there. The process, however, is not for the faint of heart. We are given a choice numerous times a day, week, month, year and throughout our lifetime. The choice to hang on, fix, repair, triage or the choice to let go, release it, and allow it to clear space for something better. I can't speak for you, but I myself am a recovering hanger-oner, refusing to accept what is and choose surrender.

The burn phase lasted a total of five years. The fire ignited on the morning of my 33rd birthday and it went out on the morning of my 38th. I remember waking up on June 16, 2023, taking my journal outside in the sun and writing for two hours. I left with an unfamiliar lightness. I'm not sure if I could pinpoint a time in my life where I felt so light. I felt free. I wasn't financially free (I'm still working on that) but I was free from the weight I had been carrying around made of all these different versions of me that weren't really me. I had spent that last five years purging through lifetimes of trauma. My physical, spiritual and energetic houses were getting cleaned up, and it was my job to buckle up and let it go. Hindsight is 20/20, of course.

Each and every time something faded away, it was a death. Death of my relationship, my dream of being a wife. Death of a career, a city, my home. The list goes on. If I wasn't comfortable with death then, I was certainly getting comfortable with it now! Letting go is an ending, and endings are forms of death. Even the end of a day, the end of a party, or the end of a year are all deaths. As humans, we are so uncomfortable with death we can't get out of its presence faster if we tried! It makes sense. We were created for life. We crave life. We do everything we can to extend it. When faced with death, we crumble. But what if we could surrender into it? What if we could believe that with every death, a new life emerges? What if we could know deep down in our souls that each time we let something go we're making space for something better? I talk a lot about death and endings in my yoga classes. It is a goal of mine to get y'all a bit more comfortable with the notion of letting go, letting things die and getting better with endings. You can't control it, so why keep fighting it? Can you trust that something better is on its way in? Faith is what finally rooted me in surrender. I was beginning to have faith that God was leading me through his divine, perfect plan for my life. I was never promised to like it all, but the less I gripped to what was, the more pleasantly surprised I became with what is.

If only God didn't speak in such a coded language. If only someone in my ethereal tribe would have told me while I was sitting in that hospital room that everything was going to fall apart, but also everything that was about to happen would be for the greater good of my soul. I wish they had told me that it was going to be five years, but it could be less if I would just let go and release control.

During my burn period I read many books, two of which stand out. Both were written by Pema Chodran: *When Things Fall Apart* and *Comfortable with Uncertainty*. Despite drinking in the wisdom, I still fought it. Surrender was such a foreign concept and I had not yet realized Yoga could be the catalyst to get me acclimated to the process of letting go. Looking back I wish I could have recognized my life going up in flames. Perhaps I would have felt more gratitude for it or heck, thrown a few more things into the smoke!

Like all thorough wildfires there are after-burns that aid in providing ample cleanout of the soil—catching all that might have been missed in the main event. This was true for mine too. Waking up on June 16, 2023, I knew things felt different and were going to get better. The smoke was starting to clear and I was able to see more than a few inches in front of me. I could feel the energy shifting, validating my knowing that opportunities were on the horizon and I was gently being lifted from the embers and ashes. It's not an overnight job coming out of such a burn. Releasing is big, spiritual work. My subconscious was working overtime to pave a cleaner road ahead. With my relief came my ability to feel even more deeply into myself, and the main feeling I was left with was pure exhaustion.

That's the thing about trauma. There may be one central event, but the aftershocks also leave a fair amount of destruction in their wake. Trauma strikes like a nuclear bomb, initiating a domino effect of casualties including people, habits, patterns, attachments, and entire communities. You were the person you were before the incident and the person you are after. Like it or not, you're forever changed. I wasn't given a choice in the matter. Fighting it and resisting the new version of me I was invited into would have been a fatal mistake. So I didn't fight it. I surrendered and stepped blindly into the light of what was ahead. To my credit, I was learning along the way and finally started to not only know, but to feel my life happening for me, and not to or against me.

One thing I know to be true is if I didn't go through what I did with my fiancé I wouldn't be where I am today. If my whole entire world hadn't fallen apart and burned to the ground, I might still be living a superficial life of social clubs, VIP lists and boating parties. I would be hiding behind a mask as a chameleon, blending in where I needed to in order to maintain relevance. I would be chasing more—more clients, more money, more dates—all because I had a void. A void I couldn't reach to fill because it was continuously covered up by all the security blankets that come with complacency. I would be traveling further away from who I was to be the person everyone else wanted me to be—the person I *thought* I wanted to be.

So often we hear,

"I just need to get back to myself."

I love how this is said in such a nonchalant way. Like we're going to go out for a walk around the neighborhood and return to our authentic selves. This is the work, people. For me, I had to release the physical stuff, and to clear out my home so there was actually space. The space gave me a way to feel, emotionally and energetically, what was actually happening in my life. Processing through the emotions, well that's no easy task and not an overnight job. It's a consistent practice. It takes yoga, meditation, sound baths, and journaling. It also takes prayer and faith. There are so many modalities, all of which are in my rotation, that can be used to emotionally let go and achieve energetic lightness. When everything is lit on fire, the stakes become pretty high to tap into the work so you don't run back in trying to save, grip and attach. In summary, it's what your yoga teacher means by letting it go. It's not for you if it's up in flames.

We can't phone in this kind of deeply transformational work. We have to practice, to be willing to let go, over and over again. It's an active choice we must make daily to loosen our grip and release what's not working. Even if we want it to work, we drop the stubborn attitude of "should" and release into surrender. We double down on our process, trade fear for more faith and are willing to walk away from the person we thought we knew in order to step into the person we are meant to be. We're being asked to upgrade, to grow and evolve all the time. I see so much resistance around this work. The resistance is the blockages, the mindsets rooted in a lack mentality and the inability to emotionally release and connect. Staying as is, in a complacent mindset without letting go is a direct line to a dumpster fire you can't even imagine. I know because I've been there. You don't have to sit stuck until the flames push you out. There are far more gentle ways to release your old self while you're in the process of stepping into who God is calling you to be.

I have always had a close relationship with my parents, and I can tell you they hardly recognized me when this transformation began taking shape. I was stepping into my purpose, my wings were spread, and I was just *different.* I think they struggled a little bit because it was such a departure from the adult child they had gotten to know steadily over the last eighteen years. When I moved to California I landed in Palm Desert, taking over the casita attached to my parent's home. To this day, when I'm in the desert this is where I live. They've watched this new person emerge, not quite knowing who she is or who she was becoming. Heck, I barely knew her and I *was* her. While I was still getting to know me in my new light, who I was becoming felt right. I knew this was authentically who I am and I continually ground myself in that feeling.

I know in my soul I will never go through another phase in my life like what I went through in those five years. I learned early on in my yoga teaching career that you should never share something you haven't processed through. I've processed through so much of my life it feels lovely to ink these fresh pages with my story. I also learned no one wants to hear your whole life story while in Warrior 2 pose. Noted! Hence why I wrote a book.

The burn phase is one of the most profound periods of time I will ever have. The first two years of it I have very little memory of. One thing I acutely recall is that from the moment the calendar year struck 2019, I started to fully withdraw. I hunkered down with all the reading material to begin my yoga teacher training and started my journey of self-discovery and healing. The training was only about six months, but my reclusion was about eighteen months. I lovingly dubbed it my soul dive—the point in time where I took myself out of the ring of life to heal. The funny thing about it is, I was planning on doing all the healing and then emerging this entirely fresh new, fully healed human ready for her real husband. Oh how the healing hadn't quite taken shape yet!

No one told me I had to hit pause and stop living while I was learning and healing. It was out of my own lack of self love that I benched myself from my life. I felt so much guilt, shame, remorse and sadness after my experience with my fiancé and all the toxic nonsense

I resorted back to as a result. I just wanted all of that to go away before I went back out into the world. But that's not how it works. We are worthy of love even while we are healing. I didn't know that, and at the time wouldn't have believed it. I do believe it now. I believe fully that the man I am supposed to be with, my forever person, is going to love me through my shadows, honor my flaws, and be the stable grounding rod in his full masculinity that I've been looking for.

I can tell you it is not necessary to spend eighteen months on the bench and years upon years in the dumpster fire in order to heal. You can keep moving, and keep living. Allow the lessons that are coming your way to land in your tissues so you don't keep reaching for the old patterns and soul-sucking security blankets. The deeper the wound, the more times you'll have to release. It's not a quick fix and there are no shortcuts. I tried many, and suffice it to say, the best gifts were practice and time. Take my advice here. If it feels like your life is on fire, why are you running back inside? Let it go. Let it burn. What is meant for you will find you. And it will find you faster if you surrender. So loosen your grip.

I'm in a beautiful place spiritually and energetically now. My faith has stood unimaginable tests and I've doubled down, rooted myself in the fact that Jesus has my back and my angels are working overtime to support me on my purposeful path. I was supposed to be in Southern California; it was my mission, my dharma to open Soul Dive Yoga. It was my divine purpose to say yes and accept the calling. And I'm so glad I did. To create a space for people to come through the door to simply be and experience their own soul dive is such a gift. And one that wouldn't have been possible if I were still hanging on with a deathgrip to the creature comforts that kept me lukewarm inside all those years ago. At the moment, we are never given the full picture of why. That's why they call it faith! Blind faith. The fear of the unknown makes us stomp out any sparks that might be igniting to take us to a bigger and better place. Stop putting them out. Fan the flame, cue Usher and let it burn.

Chapter 9
Gut and God

Our hearts know what we want, what we are destined for, what our purpose here on earth looks like. It's only through surrender can we fully arrive.

Let's get really honest here. I could tell you all the flowery things about starting over and how much I love living in California. So much sunshine and the beach—it's the land of the eternal young, wild and free! But I won't do that because it wouldn't be true. Starting over doesn't have to look like a cross-country move. It did for me, but I'm not everyone. If a move does happen to be your path, let's level-set some expectations here and get honest. Moving as a grown adult is hard. Making friends mid and even post pandemic was a challenge. Learning where to go, finding a yoga studio to call home, and becoming familiar with the nuances each city inevitably has is equal parts exciting and exhausting. Leaving my old life in Chicago was in no uncertain terms the right thing to do, but it was painfully hard to walk away from so many things I loved, not to mention the uncertainty that awaited.

"Starting over is a soulful act of bravery."

I said that as I was launching Soul Dive Yoga in October of 2022. When I first relocated to California in May of 2020 it was for a job—a job that went south and quickly ended up in a sexual harassment lawsuit. Despite the rocky start, California was still calling. So I pressed on, let go and let God take over the plan. It was during the six weeks I was back in Chicago preparing to officially leave when I was connected to another startup. I accepted the Chief Marketing Officer position and was the company's first official hire. I took a nice cash and equity package and had plans to work remote with regular visits to the headquarters in Des Moines, Iowa.

When I started my work with this company the product was merely an idea. There was no brand, no storyline and it wasn't really real yet. That's my sweet spot—taking companies from idea to market through marketing, branding and communications. I led the charge with a wonderful agency and in nine months I had a fully developed brand. It was through this experience that I learned one really big thing about my skillset. I was highly intuitive and I had an inner knowing that was showing up in my professional life. I had never heard of intuition being used in a corporate setting before and yet I was doing it. What I may have lacked in industry knowledge I made up for with my other experience. Coupled with my strong intuition, I had the ability to play in bigger conversations, more powerful rooms and make smart, strategic recommendations because I simply *knew*. If you're reading this, head nodding, don't ignore that. Your gut is powerful and I have no doubt you *know*, too.

I realize this concept could get me laughed out of rooms, but mark my words. I make business decisions from intuition every single day and I know how to teach you to do it too—just not in this book. My path to opening Soul Dive Yoga has two central themes: Surrender and Intuition. Yes, I have experience to back it all up. But your resumé is not your secret sauce and your credentials don't play as big of a role in your work as you might think. This is my opinion; you don't have to like it. If you're Ivy educated and this is triggering, double click on it. Ask yourself how you really came to know all you do. It seems these days by the time we read the textbooks the information is outdated. We know by experience, through connecting, informing through history as well as existing out in the wild. We don't just know through the black and white (the traditional testing methods leave little to be desired), but we know when our bodies light up. We can feel the knowing happen. It's a "full body yes" feeling. That feeling exists in all of us, the intuitive knowing. But we have to practice it, to get familiar with how it shows up in our physical bodies and actively work to release the self-doubt and second guessing that often arise with decision making.

When I moved to California, I relocated to my parent's home in Palm Desert as a stop-over while I figured out where I wanted to be. My tour de California lasted about a year until I landed on a beautiful little spot in Solana Beach. I went under contract sight unseen and closed in December 2021. By the first of the year I committed all of my pennies to renovating the place and was getting excited about starting over in my new little beach pad in this adorable seaside community, working remotely for a growing company with massive potential. Like all great plans, this one was better in theory. I was fired on February 17, 2022.

I happened to be in Des Moines for work on the day it happened. I was traveling back to California that morning and I remember waking up feeling resistant to get on the plane. California didn't feel like home just then and call me crazy, but I love the winter months in the midwest. I was about to get picked up for the airport when the call came in. It wasn't all that surprising when I think about it. And it further solidified that California was in fact where I was supposed to be. Validation is powerful. I was in a place where I recognized my resistance to get on the plane wasn't because I love negative twenty degree weather. It was because California was inviting me into growth. Getting fired in that moment, feeling resistance in my body to go back west, challenged my faith. I had my word of the year and this was the time to apply it. I surrendered, got on the plane and stepped into a massive growth portal on my path to opening Soul Dive Yoga.

The founder of the company I was fired from and I had become oil and water. He suffered a severe form of founder's syndrome from the get go. Founder's Syndrome, if you're not familiar, is the epitome of control, attachment and heightened emotional responses to any kind of criticism. (For being quite common, I've yet to learn of a cure other than a practice to step out of the ego and back into reality.) Founders who struggle the most tend to hire a staff that placate their wishes, who tend to not push back on their ideas and ultimately who allow the business to fizzle into the ground unless someone steps in to right the ship. I've seen it countless times over the course of my career, especially in the philanthropic space.

Despite my relationship with the founder, I loved the business and still think the idea is gold. The market is ripe for it and there was, and likely is, still a clear pathway to success. For these reasons and more, I was quite honest about all the ways his idea wasn't going to work when it showed up in real life. When you're dialed into a company in its infancy there is no need to sugarcoat the truth. Doing so leads to squandered time and treasure. Not to toot my own horn too much, but I was right. While my feedback was constructive, what he likely heard was,

"Your baby is ugly."

If there was bad news, it would be that I was out. The good news, I took four percent of my equity with me. I am, and will remain, optimistic there will be a lucrative exit!

In a stroke of divine intervention, when I was fired I had a lease sitting in my inbox to the space that is now Soul Dive Yoga. I had a few acquaintances in the desert encourage me to open a studio because most studios closed during Covid, and I know how to run a business. I was connected with a woman who owns a prime strip of real estate on El Paseo and after a casual conversation, she delivered the lease to my inbox. I hadn't even opened it yet, but it was the first thing I did when I learned I was fired.

The whole scenario was like God shouting at me, "You're going to do this!" I shouted back,

"Wait, here? In the desert?" And he said,

"Yep, here in the desert."

I surrendered. How much more clear could he have been? I had so many questions and virtually no answers. Like, "Why me?" for starters, and then of course the biggest one, "How could you lead me to make this expensive purchase on the bluff in Solana Beach?"

I'll be really honest about another thing. I had absolutely no intention, ever, even in the days where I was full blown in love with teaching yoga, of owning a studio. Sure I got a little curious, but I was never actually planning on it. For starters, the profit margin is pretty awful. And even more, I had absolutely no plan to stay in the desert. Zero, none. It's God's waiting room, why would I want to live there? But I was divinely called into this work and I am so damn grateful I was. I get these little hints I'm supposed to shake up the business of yoga, to breathe some fresh life into it. We'll see how it all pans out.

In February of 2022 I had a massive redirect. Given this wasn't my first divine redirect I was a bit more well-versed on how to play it. First and foremost, don't fight it. Remember, my word for that year was surrender. How funny, my white flag was forced up within six weeks of the new year. I went from soon-to-be beach dweller to desert business owner. I accepted the call and doubled down on all of it, firmly committed to opening Soul Dive in October, prior to the busy season kicking in. With a little grit and a lot of God, we made it happen.

We start over all the time in life. It's not always to the degree of moving across the country and opening a new business in a city you barely know, but the more we do it the more comfortable we get with it. It starts with letting go, allowing the thing that came before to die so we have room for what's new. When I moved to California it was both incredible to think about all the newness coming in and daunting to see all the uncertainty that lay ahead. I was expecting uncertainty in the forms of new friendships, routines, yoga studios and grocery stores. You know, the normal stuff we are unsure about until we really get boots on the ground in our new surroundings. But, to say the least, I was dealt a much bigger hand!

My life shifted from Chicago's social scene to California homebody. I intended to align with a local community in my new town, but instead I was tasked with creating one two hours away. I became a founder again, a role that is such a gift, but also quite isolating.

"It's lonely at the top," they say... And man, I really feel that.

All of this change happened while layers of my life were still shedding. It was like the neverending release where I had to let every single thing I knew and identified with fade away in order to step into the upgraded, Alex 2.0 version of myself.

While the guts had to spill on the table for the glory to prevail, it's not all rainbows and butterflies. I find myself on the other side full of clarity, vigor and drive to bring a God-sized vision to life. I knew when I was opening the studio it was just the beginning. I knew it needed to come first, but I didn't know *why*. I trusted my intuition and kept delivering. It turns out I was right. Soul Dive Yoga is the beginning, the foundation for what's to come to be built upon. The more I surrender into my purpose the more that gets revealed. This book (and the ones to follow) happen to be front and center of the divine plan. Apparently I have some work to do!

I trust divine timing and my intuition fully. I've always had blind faith. I know I landed where I was supposed to be, at the helm of a beautiful business and community in Palm Desert. And while that's all lovely, it has become clear that is not where I'm supposed to stay. I'm not sure if the plan is ever fully complete or the vision fully realized. I like to put a bow on things, wrap 'em up all nice and call it done. But I finally learned it doesn't work that way. Things are always shifting, evolving and changing—because we are always growing. It is our responsibility to continue letting go so we can ride the waves of change with more grace and ease. When we do, we grow. If we stop the growth, that's it. We're dead.

Some things aren't here yet and at the top of the list of what's still coming, and taking its sweet ass time by the way, is my home. I've built a community with Soul Dive, but I'm not rooted in my own community yet. I'm supposed to be here for a little bit, but is it where I put down roots? A part of me will always be connected to the desert. The mountains hold me in a way I've never felt in any geographical area. I love them; they ground me and help bring my nervous system down into a calmer state of ease and rest.

While this may not be where I root, it has yet to be revealed where that place might be. I understand living a life in surrender is the way, but I'll be the first to admit I don't always like it. And trust me, right now I don't. I miss my home. I had a beautiful home in Chicago for the last eight years I was there. I miss connections and friendships which I simply don't have in the same way that I did in Chicago. Perhaps this is a period in my life where I'm not supposed to have those things. I have to trust that. I have to know that it's not because I'm not worthy, but perhaps it's because I'm growing at such a rapid rate, I haven't found my tribe quite yet. It's okay to grow out of relationships. There is no need to light them on fire; you can simply continue evolving while gently letting them go.

Sometimes it's a really tough pill to swallow that I had to give up my home, which I was oh so attached to in Chicago, to make way for this whole soul evolution. It's been four years since the move and I don't have a real home in California yet. I live with my parents in the desert and as for the beach, it became a part-time rental property when the studio became a reality. As I pen this, I'm thirty-eight years-old, I don't know where to have my mail sent and I live in a perpetual, transient state of having at least one bag packed at all times. I know it's coming, but the waiting is more purgatory I am invited to accept!

We get put in these purgatory seasons, set down on the bench, in the space between where we were and where we are going. It's maddening, really. It has happened more times that I can count since my life fell apart on June 16, 2018. We are always placed in the liminal space for a reason. When we aren't getting what we want it's because something better is coming our way. I believe that. I personally lack patience and even just writing that I feel like a fraud. I behave more like Moses slapping his staff on the rock demanding God show up for me. But if I paused and looked around, I would see how insanely abundantly blessed my life is and has been.

The space in between tests our faith; liminal spaces show up equally whether your shit is burning to the ground or you're on the rise building your empire out of the ashes. Either way, you're being tested. You're being asked to wait. I started hearing my angels speak to me a few years ago. These were actual voices I would hear in my head that no one else would hear. I remember the first time it happened, I was standing at an intersection in Encinitas. In that particular town the lights turn for each traffic pattern then all cars stop and the people can cross in all ways, including diagonally. When you're at the crosswalk and you hit the button and it's not time to go, a voice will say,

"Wait."

The first time I was at the crosswalk and heard the voice, I knew it. I had heard that voice before. The voice had been in my head numerous times and it dawned on me. All those times I was forcing my life to go a certain way, I was being asked to wait.

I hear "Wait" a lot to this day, and it is the same voice that informs the pedestrians in Encinitas. But lately, the voice has evolved a bit. Instead of just wait, I now hear,

"Stop, collaborate and listen."

Do you know what that's from? It's the song "Ice Ice Baby" by Vanilla Ice. I can't make this stuff up. (For more hoobajup stuff that sounds made up, get to the next two chapters—oh my!) So now, I'm supposed to wait, collaborate and listen. So I surrender. I release the need to force an outcome or accelerate a timeline that isn't divine yet. I simply wait, and when more is needed, I stop, collaborate and listen.

When we start living outside of our purpose, which will happen to each and every human on earth likely multiple times during their lifetime, we accumulate layers that make us deaf. It makes it harder to hear the alignment, the redirects and the invitations to get back to you and why you're here. As the layers shed we become more receptive, acute listeners. We're more equipped to respond.

There are only two things that make this possible, and they are Gut and God. Gut is your intuition. While I do think women have a more heightened sense of knowing, men have it too. Men are just denser creatures that require more kneading to condition the intuition. Your gut speaks to you all day. The feelings of hunger, thirst, nervousness, and anxiety are all felt in the gut, or sacral area, if you want to talk subtle (or energetic) body. If we start in the physical, what we consume goes directly into the gut in an effort to nourish the body. What we eat matters. I spent the better part of my adult life eating salads, grains, raw vegetables, and consuming food prepared at restaurants undoubtedly cooked in seed oils and other disgusting ingredients. I even went so far as to explore the vegan diet. I nearly died. I couldn't stand, my brain wouldn't function and I was experiencing a system shutdown like none other. I thought I was supposed to eat salad to stay thin. While I did stay thin, I was perpetually bloated, belly distended and digestive track constantly upset. It's easy to blame IBS when most of the population thinks they are diagnosed with some condition or allergy. While I am not a doctor or a nutritionist (of which I think both are under-educated and have a narrow focus on symptom management, which is far more profitable than solving the issue), food was making me chronically sick. And it's doing so to many people in this country.

My relationship with food was never a problem. I was a fat kid, remember? I would eat anything. I over consumed, and as a child, I don't recall whether or not my stomach had issues. As a young adult, I was constantly sick. My stomach pain was debilitating, often sending me home mid-dinner because I couldn't sit upright. I was consuming foods that were poisonous to my system. I thought I had all kinds of allergies, dairy for one (I was never educated that it might be pasteurized dairy that was the culprit for my sensitivity), and I even went so far as to say I was intolerant to sauces and flavor. What kind of bullshit is that? I was suffering from the food choices and the ingredients in which my food was prepared. Modern medicine won't be able to get to the bottom of that, trust me.

For years I was encouraged to move to a carnivore diet, which consists of high animal fat consumption, butter and dairy. This also involved releasing salad, specifically greens like spinach and kale (which are completely toxic to your system), removing grains and nuts and going back to a real milk latte. Can we just take a moment for how delicious a latte tastes with half and half? My mind was blown by this invitation. It went against everything I was taught.

"Eat your veggies," they said.

Which should have come with a toxicity warning label that your gut would be destroyed. Ever wonder why people do celery juice cleanses? Because the contents of their insides empty out. And people (mostly women) continue on the juice path because they still "look fat!" Well that might be true, because when you irritate a part of your body to no end you become inflamed, bloated and experience the distended belly I did for so many years. If I could end one thing it would be veganism. We are primal beings meant to consume animal products. Responsibly sourced, grass fed, happy cows are of course best, but grain finished cattle are still healthier than most other things humans choose to eat.

I finally made my way over to the carnivore diet when I couldn't stand it anymore. I had been attacked by my food one too many times so I was ready to give it a try. At first I dipped my toe in the water. Steak and a salad! Nope, there it was again, the salad causing my stomach to churn and remain bloated. It's not easy going against what you've been told since you were a kid. But I finally did it. I have been actively eating this way for three years. Beef and butter baby! And you know what? I've never looked or felt better. My body appears as though I spend hours in the gym. I don't. I hate working out. I go for a nice walk and do a little yoga. That's it folks. If you were to have told me a chaturanga was a burpee I never would have gone to yoga in the first place! My face looks more youthful thanks to the collagen intake through my food choices. I supplement with organs and my brain function has increased. There have been absolutely no downsides. My favorite, outside of looking and feeling amazing, is how easy it is to eat this way. I don't have to source some special fake ingredient that costs a fortune; I can show up to my local grocery store, grab the 10 ounce New York and a sweet potato and dinner is ready in thirty minutes.

I could get on my diet soapbox and stay there forever. Here's why it matters. If the belly is the source of our feeling and our gut, the literal connection to our intuition, keeping it clean is essential. What you consume has the ability to block, as much as it has the ability to open your gateway to listening to the divine. When your gut is full of sugar a few things happen. First, there is a trigger to your brain and you go into fight or flight. It's igniting your adrenaline, signaling there might be something wrong. After the spark-up there's a crash. Our mental health takes a dip and we seep into a place where our thoughts are not disciplined or managed. Some may experience depression, others more irrational or erratic thinking patterns. I would be lying if I said I don't eat sugar anymore. I do eat it and am the first to admit if the dessert is worth having, my fork is the first one in. But I'm aware of what's going on. I know the physical response and I can implement some tools to manage the side effects of my consumption choices.

When the gut stays clear, healthy and aligned our systems can be at ease. When our basic needs are met—like quality food intake, sleep and rest—we can actually come back down into our bodies instead of the manic symptom management brought on by our consumption. When our guts are healed we have the ability to listen better; we step into a higher vibration in optimal health that wasn't possible on foods that are anti-nutrient and toxic to our systems. It's essential to pay attention to what goes in so we can hear what's coming through. It's a direct connection, gut and God, and I've experienced firsthand what happens when we create a clear pathway for the messages to come through from the divine.

God is your messenger. The God I speak about and am rooted in is Jesus. I must say, we all need more Jesus. He will speak to you. His messengers come in so many ways, shapes and forms. It's not as black and white as a figure of a man with a beard and booming voice visiting you in your bedroom. God speaks through his angels, the ethereal tribe as I like to call them. They communicate through numbers, images and signs, codes and symbols. If you're asleep you'll surely miss it. Unless of course you're being talked to in your dreams. God sends messages in human forms as well. It could be an astrologer, a random man on the street, or the woman in the checkout line. God is constantly talking to us. I can't help but wonder where my life would be if I could listen to even half of what he's saying. But I do my best. It's noisy upstairs! Our minds are constantly chatting and it's such useless information. The mental chatter of shoulds, chores, annoyances, tasks, kids, whatever the list could go on and on! We have to get quiet so we can listen.

We have to stop, collaborate and listen.

Getting quiet is the work; it's part of the practice. Whether it's yoga, meditation, journaling, a long walk, or ten minutes of quiet time in the sun it's important we figure out what works for us to discipline our thoughts. We can't control them, that I know. But we can apply discipline to get things to a quiet (or quieter) place so we have the ability to hear.

Hearing is just the beginning. Yes, first we must notice. Maybe it's a word or something we read on the internet, a series of numbers or an animal we see in our backyard day after day. Noticing is just the beginning. We are then tasked with deciphering these messages and making sense of it all. We can take to the internet and consult Google if there's a recognizable pattern, or we could seek validation from an outside source. Sure, there are many ways to double click on something you're noticing. But the way we do it, so that the messages are interpreted for us, is through our intuition. When something lands, we'll feel the alignment. Our bodies will start to move in the direction of the message and we'll just know we're heading in the right direction. God will charge his angels around you and you will be directed. It is essential that you believe and know that. God shows up for you in vast, enormous ways that we can hardly comprehend as humans. All you have to do is listen. And in some cases, stop, collaborate and listen.

Nothing about my redirect made logical sense. Move across the country, live with my parents, buy an expensive beach property, end up with a yoga studio, and the list goes on. My old self would have tried to right the ship, redirecting everything that was happening to make more logical sense. Alex 1.0 would have fought. I never would have let go and let God do his thing. I do let go now, mostly, or at least to the best of my human ability. Despite being limitless creatures, we are a bit limited when it comes to the mind and understanding what's happening in our lives, and the work we do to make sense of it all. When we release the need to know, we can loosen our grip on controlling the outcome. It's back to the expectations, and how having them hogties our happiness to certain outcomes. Just like the vegans and their thousand item ingredient list full of alternative products that aren't real food, we over complicate the process. To break it down, I'll offer this formula.

1. Let go and let God.
2. Heal your gut, trust your intuition.
3. Talk to God, receive unimaginable love and support.

And of course, because you're human, you will fall flat from time to time and receive some divine redirects that you don't have to like, but you'll trust are for your greater good. It's the process of allowing and less pushing that we can really tap into what we want. It's then we can become powerful manifesters of our lives. None of it works if you're blocked, resist faith and respond with fear. Once you trust that your gut is your superpower, God is your kryptonite and through Jesus you'll have the glory, you can adjust your cape and embody your purpose without a shadow of a doubt you're on the right path.

Chapter 10

Happy Horseshit

If you don't move toward your manifestations it's all a bunch of happy horseshit.

If you don't move toward your manifestations it's all a bunch of happy horseshit. I believe that. And what's better, I'm surrounded by happy horseshit. I feel like the state of California, above all states, is one giant happy horseshit collective. But as much as I'd like to isolate it to California, it's everywhere. It's the dreams, the I-wants, the entitled attitude that you deserve the sun moon and stars. That it is your birthright. Look, your birthright is to have your heart's desires—but nobody said it was going to be easy and just fall in your lap. It's work.

I can take credit for the concept that if we don't move toward our manifestations it's all happy horseshit. That's totally mine. What I can't take full credit for is the use of "happy horseshit" to begin with. A few years ago while in the midst of my own Soul Dive, I remember receiving a shipment of books. I was visiting my parents in

Iowa and my dad brought the delivery outside where I was posted up. He looked at me and said,

"Alex, here's more of your happy horseshit."

I was slightly irritated by his lack of understanding, but mostly I laughed.

Back then I was in the throes of deep, introspective work at the time. I read every Pema Chodran book I could get my hands on, clinged to every word Michael Singer wrote in *Untethered Soul*, and referenced *The Road Back to You* daily (Eneagream stuff, iykyk). I started to think about what we call into our lives. . . the prayers, hopes, dreams, manifestations and cultivations. We make vision boards, answer journal prompts, and read thoughtful literature. What we do with all that content matters. If we just accumulate knowledge, does that actually enhance our lives or make us wise? Wisdom is knowledge applied. If we don't do the work to bring our visions to life, looking beyond our current complacency is a useless exercise. Our energy flows where our attention goes. So I landed on my theory: If we don't move toward our manifestations it is all a bunch of happy horseshit.

We don't get to where we're going by sitting idly on the couch or clicking our heels together three times, Dorothy. Complacency is stagnant, dead energy. I can smell it a mile away. I've promised you the truth and my authenticity, so here it goes. All those things you want—your vision boards, journal pages, hours of heartfelt conversations with friends—that's all real and I personally believe you should have each and every thing you desire. So does God. But if you don't move toward your manifestations it ain't gonna happen. What do I mean by this?

I mean you should be embodying the life you want to live as if it's here, upon you now. Say you want to move across the country.

You're not sure when, where or why. You just feel the call to go. Then nothing changes or even bigger, you keep redoing your house, buying more stuff and rooting deeper in the routines and rhythms in your current environment. I've watched this happen. People have I-wants, but they never do anything about them. Stop whining and start living! This is one of the biggest examples of blocked energy. If I had a taboo buzzer to ding over the pages I would hit it. Now I don't have all the answers, but I do have this one.

It became clear I needed to leave Chicago a couple years before I actually went. When I felt the urge, I started to purge. Beginning with my closet, my friend (the famed stylist) came over and supported the mission. Dozens of bags of clothing that no longer served me, didn't fit, out of date—gone. She helped me release countless pieces I had been hanging on to, some even since college. Why? Did I think I couldn't rebuy an item if I missed it? No. I shopped all the time. I was shoving old stuff in the corners of my house and it was keeping me stuck. I would reorganize by folding things so small I could fit all the new stuff in. I never knew what to wear because I didn't even know what was there. What's more, I was pushing myself further and further into the corners of the life I wanted to move away from. When I finally started letting go, the floodgates opened up.

Once California revealed itself as the destination, I was committed to moving with next to nothing. Not only did my house sell to the first woman that walked through it, but all the furniture I listed got scooped up within days. I'll never forget the lovely people who came through to pick up my bedroom set, office furniture and more. It was a lifegiving moment to know that the things I loved and made my house so beautiful went on to serve a new family.

I kept going with the release, unloading the darkest corners of my home and selling, donating, or gifting everything I didn't use on a daily basis. Have you lived somewhere for eight years? I bet you have. How do your closets look? The amount of stuff I had did not reflect a single woman with a tiny dog! I watched my stuff fly out the window so quickly it just validated my decision to go. Sure, it was a little scary. But energetically speaking, all the things, the stuff, the dead stagnant energy had to get away. I was committed to removing anything that could have held me back.

When I got settled out West in the desert I remember my mom walking into my closet, horrified. She went on and on about how I didn't have any clothes. For the first time in my life my closet had space. I could see between pieces. I could move things around without stuffing. I begged her not to shop for me. If I'm honest, a small piece of me didn't want anything because I was still a bit resistant to wearing actual pants post pandemic. When you retire jeans for so long, it's a little hard to stuff your body back into the denim. But mostly, I didn't want anything because I didn't think I was staying. I was still in my process of evolving and I didn't want to be hauling around a bunch of stuff. As I am still here, it's clear I was wrong and it likely won't be the last time.

To date, I can put all of my personal belongings in my car. I might have to put the dog on my lap and use the front seat, but it will all fit. Not the furniture, but the stuff. Clothes, shoes, jewelry, handbags—all of it. I'm insanely proud of this. My mindset shifted to knowing I can provide for myself when I need it. I know that if I want a nice piece of clothing I can afford it. I believe I can buy a few really nice pieces and have a super edited wardrobe and always know what I'm wearing. Let's just say, hypothetically speaking, the man of my dreams says one day that we have to move to Paris. Alex 1.0 would take months to be ready. Alex 2.0 needs maybe 48 hours and a private jet for her dog… just sayin'. This is some serious freedom, people!

The point is this: If I hadn't started letting go, I might never have left. If I hadn't started clearing space, I might not have had the space to bring in the new opportunity that essentially took me out West. Space is required so we can have a place to allow aligned opportunities to land. Without space we have nowhere for the new to go. It tries to come in, but is quickly rerouted. We have to be ready. And getting ready is a constant practice. Numerous times in my life I haven't been ready. I sure as heck wasn't ready for the diagnoses my fiancé received on my birthday. I wasn't ready for the fallout I was about to experience on the heels of it all. But those experiences sparked something inside of me that I needed to not only *get* ready, but *be* ready. Once it did, I was inspired to share.

We are so ill-equipped to cope with life. Seriously, something happens and we crumble, fall apart unsure how to put the pieces back together and unwilling to let the old pieces go. Purging is at the top of my list when it comes to getting ready. Purge negative thoughts, purge toxicity, purge people, and purge your sacred spaces. Once you start releasing you will be amazed at the space you create for the newness to arrive. The newness could also be labeled as change, which is why energetically I think people are so accustomed to resisting it. We don't know what's new because we haven't had it yet. Can we lean on our faith and surrender into knowing it's better than what we had?

There are a lot of people that live in a complacent mindset, stuck. They want all the things—a life partner, more money, a bigger house. But their condo is decorated with their grandmother's furniture. Do you see how one negates the other? Then there is the person who a deeper relationship with their partner but refuses to .d college T-shirts or unpack the boxes that are still taped .neir move four years ago. They're stuck. Please don't be that person that says you'll go through your stuff when you move into the next house. Please! It's not fair to the new house, your spouse or you. Do the work now. Even if you're not planning on going anywhere, clean up your house! Why? Because you need to be ready for what's to come. I don't know what that is for you or when it will hit, but I know your life will always be shifting and changing, unless you stifle it. And lord knows we as humans can be good and that.

If you're a Bible girl like me you know this: God tells us to get ready because we don't know when he's coming back (I'm paraphrasing that one). It is written all over the Bible to get our affairs in order. And on the other end of the spectrum, there is Abraham Hicks, American author, motivational speaker and channeler. She has a bit in her "Infinite Awakening" spoken word piece that says we need to be ready to be ready to be ready to be ready to be ready for whatever it is we need to be ready for. But how? Where do we start? The questions swirl around, I know. It's overwhelming to think about preparing for the thing we don't know is coming. It starts with faith, rooted steadfast in the fact that what's coming is bigger, better and more purposeful than what you had before. To get there, we need a practice and that, my friends, is where the work comes in.

I'm just sharing my experience here; this is not a self help book. I can tell you my next book is already in the works and there is a massive emphasis on clearing out the bowels of your life. (So get a head start and hit your closets.) If you ask yourself whether you should keep something and your answer is maybe, let it go. I feel passionately about this one and get struck by anxiety when I see clutter in anyone's home. Especially the home of someone I love and care about, and might be considering a future with. Know this, if I'm dating you and you have any of the following: old T-shirts, clothes that don't fit, beaten up shoes, dust collected on anything and unpacked boxes anywhere in your home, I'm out. What I see is a scarcity complex, lack of self-worth, stuck in a complacent mindset and no awareness. It's too much for me to fix, even if I was willing to try. You might be thinking,

Why don't you do it for me if you're so good at it?

I could, and it wouldn't take me more than a few days to get your physical space in shipshape. But let me anchor this in you: It is not my work to do. It's yours. You've got to get physical with your stuff. Don't think twice, just get rid of it. Hire an organizer, give her free reign and get out of the way. Clean out your closets, tidy up your storage room and organize your junk drawer. Doing so is making room for the rest of your life.

Moving toward our manifestations is something that has become overlooked. The wellness community has made manifesting look like wishing on a shooting star. I wish that were the truth, but it's not. You have to put it in motion, to live like it's already here; write about it like you're experiencing the thing you're calling in right now. I've shared the truth about my journey. If I could have wished away my grief, sadness and fear I would have done it and saved myself years in the trenches of deep emotional healing work.

When I think back to my experience with my fiancé's diagnosis and how I responded once he left, I'm shocked by my behavior. I thought I could make the pain go away if I could just find another man to love me through it. You know how this ends, not only unsuccessful but delaying the process of healing my trauma, wounds and my own heart. I had to go through all the hurt and the pain of letting go. I had to work through the toxic patterns I had with men. This took me years. And quite frankly, it might be an area of my life that requires constant attention. When thinking about my romantic life and the deep desire I have for partnership, marriage and a family, I needed to double down on my practice.

Historically I would have made a checklist. He had to have all these characteristics or I wouldn't consider him. That's all well and good, but it's not enough. Romantic relationships can't thrive on a resumé alone. We can't apply black and white facts to emotions and feelings. There is an energetic agreement you're making with each other and if you overlook the feelings, the emotions at the root of the relationship, you're simply hiring a transient worker that will move on to a better offer. It's only a matter of time. Once I realized this, I shifted to a focus on feeling. Not just who I want to call in, but how I wanted to feel with this person. I wrote pages and pages about how I wanted to feel in his presence and in our relationship. I still revisit this tool when I'm in the mindset of calling in my forever person. This work allows me to embody it, as if he's already here.

I got clear on my emotions, embodied them, then put them in writing, taking myself on a journey through my journal as if this man is already with me. This isn't the only work I did in this department. It always goes back to releasing, letting go of what doesn't serve. I had to get out of the toxic hamster wheel and put myself on a pedestal. Once I stopped accepting less than, I was sending a message to the universe that I was ready for more. I was ready to get what I deserve because I had the tools to nurture it.

If we don't dive into the work—and let me tell you there are many ways to skin the cat here, these are just the practices that have worked for me—then it's not going to happen. Or we'll get just bits and pieces but not the whole package. If you try to shortcut the process you might get a taste and think,

Wow, that worked!

But then, poof. It's all gone. We can't skirt the truth of where we need to get dialed in. We have to lock eyes with it, to sit in the discomfort of knowing it's there and make a conscious effort to work through it. Shadow work, anyone?

I lived for years in old patterns. So much stuck energy kept me looping in my own stuff, unable to see it, let alone release it. I was doing the same thing and expecting different results. That's insane, right? I kept waiting to be saved. Time and again I looked on the horizon for my white knight. It took the 2x4 moment to wake me up and change the trajectory of my actions, to inspire a healthier mindset and put my life in a new energetic direction. Looking back I wish I would have learned sooner. I wish my twenties were spent building healthier habits and a more purposeful lifestyle. It's hard not to fall victim to regret. It's even harder to forgive myself for all those years living deaf, dumb and blind to the invitations, signs and messages that it just didn't need to be that way. But like I've already said, I'm not a subtle learner and those gentle nudges weren't going to work for me at the time.

We can go our whole lives completely fooling ourselves. We can live in the dialogue of "Everything is fine, we're good, nothing is wrong." We can make like baby boomers and sweep it all under the rug until the pile of stuff under there becomes so big we fall flat on our faces. Eventually shit will hit the fan. It's exhausting to be fine, isn't it? To paint this picture, just open your Instagram app. No matter who shows up on your feed, the images are the same. The family is good, their relationship is flawless, the house is always cleaned up. But it's not real. When we tell these perpetual white lies to the people around us, we're working overtime to convince ourselves that there's merit. But really there's no truth there. The truth comes with lifting the rug and sweeping up the dust. A little will get in your nose and you'll probably sneeze, but you took care of it. You cleaned it up.

Clean it up before it becomes a bigger problem. Don't do what I did and ignore it, waiting for your prince to come save you from yourself. He's not coming. Because he's not real. If you see him in the physical, he's a bandaid at best. Choose to put on this bandaid, and you're prolonging the inevitable nosedive you'll be forced to do in your own mess. Do you have that kind of time to waste? I don't. If you can practice getting into the corners of your physical space you will get more comfortable diving into the energetic realms. It's the practice. Start small, but the point is to start somewhere. If it scares you and it's difficult, good! It's not easy looking at your mess, but it's required. You not only have to look at it, but you have to find a way to love yourself through it. The word for this is *grace*. The work is hard; it's messy and wildly uncomfortable. But if you don't do it, if you don't get brutally honest with what lies beneath the surface, then your life becomes a bunch of happy horseshit.

Life was never guaranteed to be easy, free of conflict, hurt, pain or suffering. The promise was never happiness, unicorns and fairy dust. I wish it was. From my experience, and what I've witnessed in others, we begin complaining as soon as something goes wrong. It's the *woe is me*, victim mentality and *why is this happening to me* conversation. I don't have the tolerance for those tables anymore. Heck, I probably used to set the darn table. But not anymore. The complaining is the happy horseshit. The wishing things were different without putting one ounce of grit behind the shift is happy horseshit. The gossip, tearing down someone else to make yourself feel better, that's all happy horseshit. It's fake, insincere and destined for failure. It won't make you happy. If you are this person, hear this again. All this nonsense will not make you happy. It's time to double down on your honesty so you can live more authentically.

It's okay not to be happy. It's okay to have your whole life fall apart. In fact, it's required for things to fall apart so they break into pieces so tiny you couldn't possibly pick them up if you tried. Why? Because they are not for you. If you keep putting the old pieces back together eventually you'll end up like an outdated software system— held together with a little bit of duct tape and bubblegum. They weren't serving you, which is why they fell apart in the first place. So let it go. Allow everything to crumble that is no longer serving you, be it the job, the marriage, the city, or the friendships—all of it. Let them fall apart and allow the purge. If this sounds really dramatic to you then you need to go get in your closet and do some work, my friend. Because the more we practice letting go the easier it becomes when something really big sees its way out of your life. When the grip is already loose it falls by the wayside.

We will file this one under one of my favorite sayings,

"Let the trash take itself out."

Taylor Swift said something along these lines in her *Time* Magazine interview. As much as I love T-Swift, she wasn't the first in my world to speak it. A woman I had the pleasure of practicing yoga with in Chicago, and attended my first retreat after opening Soul Dive, said it to me on the phone one day.

"Let the trash take itself out."

Sit with that. If it's not for you it will not stay with you. So why are you hanging on with a deathgrip? My assumption is fear. Because fear is the crippling thing that comes between letting go and allowing what's new. We don't know the new, so we fear it. But what if you flipped the script and acknowledged fear as the awareness of courage? Could you bravely go forth into the unknown? I think you could. You have plenty of closets to open up and you have the tools to practice.

So make like Elsa and let it go. Save the happy horseshit for someone else. It's not for you, because you know better. I have faith in you because I was you. I was you on the bottom of the bathroom floor sobbing my eyes out wishing it would all just go away—wishing I could wake up and not hurt anymore. Hoping I would fall in love again and build a life with someone.

As I pen this book I'm six years out from when my world fell apart. I can tell you this is one of the greatest practices I've adopted and as much as it's in my tissues, rooted by my faith and never lets me down it's not easy. I've absolutely had things fall apart since the diagnosis. Plenty! I've had various relationships, personal and professional, that have gotten up and out of my orbit in a flash. The difference? I don't go chasing them anymore. If a guy shows up at my door and ends the relationship out of the blue, guess what that's filed under. Yep, let the trash take itself out. The same goes for business. When we root in our practice and are living in purpose we realize we need very little around us to thrive. In fact less really is more, and we start to feel that to be true once the practice of letting go gets more familiar. This is precisely why I invite you to start in the physical. If you can part with your worldly possessions it makes it a heck of a lot easier to part with people.

As cliché as it sounds, rejection is God's protection. Sure, your ego might take a little blow; give yourself grace for that. Instead of running back into the dumpster fire, can you simply say thank you? It's never an overnight job and takes time, intentional practice and a heck of a lot of vulnerability to sit through an unexpected blow. But someday you'll arrive in a place of equanimity where the highs and the lows don't swing the pendulum so far in either direction. We want more ease and peace in our lives. Letting go and rooting our lives in alignment with our heart's desires is the way to get there. If someone tells you this is easy, run the other way. You are not one mushroom journey away from a fully healed human. (Trust me I tried that too.) The work is in front of you for a reason, so you do it. Surrendering into your life is a full time job. So take the time to create the space and practice. We don't need any more happy horseshit on this planet. If I learned nothing else from living in California it's that this state has enough happy horseshit to last the globe a lifetime.

Chapter 11
Anger, Grief & Closure

Healing rests in accepting the ending that is presenting and the ability to be at peace while letting go.

I think most would agree death is one of the most final experiences we have as humans. When death hits, that's it. There are no more seats at the table, conversations around the fire, welcoming hugs or farewell kisses. I had been anticipating my former fiancé's death for the better part of four years. I always knew he would outlive his prognosis. He was strong, determined and had access to any and every treatment, therapy, alternative medicine and healing modality on earth. If money, resources, or additional brain power could have been thrown at his situation to extend his life, it was. But sometimes that's just not enough. In his case, it wasn't. That's the thing about death. You can't escape it if it's your time. He left his life on earth just as I was stepping more fully into mine.

He died on September 14, 2022, just over four years since his diagnosis. It was the very day I was given the keys and took possession of the space that was soon to be Soul Dive Yoga. I didn't learn of his death on that day; I was informed via text six weeks later on October 20th. It was moments after I welcomed the first group of retreat guests for Soul Dive's very first Weekender. We gathered in the studio where I served cacao and set the tone for the weekend: Eager, uplifting and ready. I glanced at my phone just as I spoke my last words to the group and saw his brother's name appear, and I knew. I really didn't need to open the text message, but I did. I saw the words,

"We lost him" across the screen and my heart fell to pieces, dropping into places in my body I didn't even think were possible. Even knowing what I was going to see paired with the anticipation I've felt for over four years wasn't going to bail me out of this one.

I stepped outside and to my own surprise, the biggest feeling I felt was freedom. I was free from worry, fear and anticipation. He was free from pain and suffering. Sadness was certainly there. How could it not be? No matter how much we know something is coming, when it actually happens we feel its permanence. There is so much sadness in all endings, especially those that end in loss. But no matter how sad I felt, freedom was the trump card. I gathered myself together and taught the first class of the retreat. I made it through the weekend, dangling by a thread, before falling apart early the following week. Once I had the space to start processing I landed smack in the middle of grief. What a terrible place, I'm not at all surprised we avoid it at all cost. But it's where we're supposed to go after loss. Maybe it's not your first step, but it's required to move forward. Some people take years to finally acknowledge the grief. I get it. But despite how awful the experience, we have to acknowledge it, feel it, live it and move on from it. Grief is a rite of passage as we continue embarking upon our human existence. Pushing it down into our bodies or further away on our timelines only delays our healing process.

My last visit with him was in June. I had gone over to his parents' home and we shared a Chicago deep dish pizza. He knew me. He told me he loved me. He knew our jokes. He told me to take it easy on his mother. I didn't know why he said this until later, after he passed. I asked him if he was ready to die yet and he said no. I believed him when he said he wasn't quite ready. I also knew he never wanted me to see him in that state, or whatever state the end was going to look like. When we were together the conversation would frequently turn dark. To lighten it up he would tell me to look hot at his funeral. We would uncomfortably laugh. I always thought I would be there, no matter what or where I was in my own life. I thought many times in my search for a partner that I would be looking for a man strong enough to attend his funeral with me. There was a part of me that looked forward to that moment. A moment of real closure, where he would look down at me, meet the man I was with and know I was cared for, happy and okay. . . All the things he wanted to do for me, but got stripped away overnight.

It didn't take long for things to turn ugly in our home after the diagnosis. There was so much fear and uncertainty, clinical information and outside influences. I had no idea how to cope and he was just trying to survive. How unfair. While we had beautiful moments together during that period there was such a darkness in the relationship, one that couldn't be fixed. I ended up walking away in what I believe to be an act of self preservation. Put your own life mask on first, then help others. I hadn't taken care of myself in months and this felt like an act of desperation. Get out, or sink. What

I believe now is this: he intentionally pushed me away during that summer when he received the diagnosis. He didn't let the relationship recover because he wanted me to save myself. Deep down he knew how bad this was going to get. I chose rose colored glasses I suppose, thinking that one day I would wake up and it would all go away. It didn't. He loved me so much that he wanted to spare me from living through what he was about to experience. He didn't want my life to fall apart, so he allowed the cloud to descend until I couldn't stand it anymore. I feel grateful to know that kind of love exists and while I wasn't aware at the time, I was receiving it.

In mid-November, just as the studio was about six weeks old, I was at the LaQuinta Farmers Market arriving at a unique vendor with hats, bags and various accessories. I bought a hat and the woman who owned the business, who had made small talk with me, looked at me and in no uncertain terms said we needed to connect. Willing to connect with anyone that showed even the slightest bit of interest in me or Soul Dive, I said of course. She was coming to breath work that night at the studio, as was I, so we planned to sort it out there. After the class she came up to me, shared her feedback on the experience and asked me one question that completely changed my life.

This woman had known me for less than twelve hours at the time. She was vaguely familiar with my story but had no clue of the intimate details. I told her my former fiancé had just passed away in September. She said,

"Okay, well he's right over there," pointing to the place where I had just been laying down for breath work and the sound bath which followed.

Part of me wanted to laugh in disbelief and just shake it off. But I knew she was right. I knew he was there. I had felt him there. I just didn't want to admit it. In fact, I usually had Alfie with me during the many long days I spent at the studio. Each and every time Alfie was free to roam he would go over to that space and just be. Sometimes he would lay down and nap, others he would stand there like someone was talking to him. Dogs know, and if we are really clear and honest with ourselves, we know too.

I clearly had a lot of questions. The next evening this woman spent hours with me, explaining her gift and walking me through the messages coming through to her. This was my first experience with the death of someone that was so close to me and outside of watching some far fetched reality shows I had never experienced a medium first hand. She said he had been contacting her, talking to her and needing to talk to me. I filled her in on the details of our story, how we met, the diagnosis, caretaking and everything in between. He was communicating with her the whole time we were together that evening. Most of what he needed to say I already knew. The love he had for me was so strong he didn't want me to suffer, to go down with him, if you will. He had been silenced for the last few years of his life as a result of his cancer manipulating his brain. His family, rightfully so, was unwilling to let him go. They were prolonging his life. I remember when I stopped hearing from him via text, at which point our communication was forced through another person. For me, seeing him the June before he passed was closure. I knew that could be the last time I saw him, and I felt at peace. But for him, there was so much more to be said and I will be eternally grateful for his perseverance.

When he died, I believe he came to find me before going to heaven. I believe the realms are so thin, but we as humans are too blocked to see, feel or explore. I felt him there and once it was confirmed, I didn't want him to leave. When I would show up to the studio to teach, I was comforted by his presence. We were nearly in a lawsuit with the landlord because the tenant upstairs was complaining about music that would play at all hours of the night. I had to politely ask him to stop playing records and turning on the music. I know it was him. The records were from our engagement party and were so deeply personal to both of us. We had dreams of a beautiful home, a stunning record player, vinyls decorating the space around it and quiet moments sipping our house cocktail, which consisted of Koval bourbon, orange LaCroix, and an orange slice. Before he was diagnosed, we would start our weekend around 5:30 p.m. every Friday evening, after I went to yoga and when he returned home from work. He would make us a cocktail and we would just connect. Sometimes we would never leave the couch, others we'd enjoy a nice date night out on the town. It wouldn't matter what we did, we just wanted to spend the entire weekend together, the two of us. Our time was too short on this side of glory and I haven't had one of those cocktails since he left.

In a way I was dating my dead fiancé again. When I was there by myself I knew he was with me. I could feel his presence. It was a level of intimacy I might never know again. I know how it sounds and lord help me, I wish sometimes it wasn't the case. But it was. He died and came to Soul Dive Yoga. My teachers felt it, those that are really in touch. And most of all, my body felt it. There were certainly sweet moments where I felt him by my side, but physically my body was starting to feel and process through all of the grief I had stored up for years. Even though I had painfully sat waiting by the phone for the news of his passing, anticipating his death, I couldn't pre-process the grief. It wasn't until he did die that I was able to arrive in the grief. Even with his soul there, holding my hand through the thin veils that differentiate our dimensions, I was breaking down. I had been there before, the place where you have to completely fall apart before you can get up again. When it finally came, his death, we got to be together again. It's sad, tragic even, but so beautiful. Yes, it's got *Ghost* vibes all over it, but it was quite real.

One of the questions I asked the medium was how long he would stay. While she didn't have that information, and in the context of this conversation time was completely elusive, she shared some meditations I could practice to help him feel ready to move on. He had a strong faith rooted in Jesus. So do I. He knew the Kingdom of Heaven waited for him and he just needed to let go to fully arrive. Apparently it was my job to help him do so. You just never know when your next resumé builder will show up.

I was teaching on a Wednesday evening and as always, had a candle lit in the bathroom. As we were wrapping up class and closing down the studio one of my teachers asked if I wanted her to blow it out. I said no, I would do it before I left. Once I got home I was sitting in the hot tub, looking up at the stars. My exhaustion was weighing on me, my body aching. The stress of a new business, death, grief, uncertainty, all of it was piling on my shoulders. As I sat soaking, looking up at the stars, I was met with a ping that I forgot to blow out the candle. The ping came immediately with his face. My mind was holding the two together in space. It was as clear of an invitation as receiving one in the mail.

Come back, I'm ready to go.

I knew I was supposed to go back that night. I knew he was inviting me. Still I resisted. I texted my teaching team asking if someone was in the area with a key so they could take care of the candle. They weren't. And I knew they wouldn't be.

I showered, considered hair and makeup—I mean there is no rule book for saying goodbye to your late fiancé between realms—defaulted to cozy and returned to the studio. I had no idea what I was walking into. This was my first experience with this kind of loss. The entire drive my energy was heavy, sad and full of dread. I just knew I had to walk in and blow out the candle. How hard is that? But I knew it was him talking to me, and I knew he was saying goodbye.

I parked out front and let myself in the studio. Immediately looking to my right I knew he was there, sitting on his cushion in the corner. I told him how much I loved him. I thanked him profusely for coming to see me, grateful he was able to see the beautiful space I built, that's serving so many people and was inspired by our relationship, shared experience and deep love. I told him how happy I was that he got his closure. Grateful that all of the pain we went through together was an effort to spare me of more heartache. There wasn't anything else to be said or done. I told him it's okay to go and that I'd love to see him from time to time, thankful that he would become one of my angels and check on me as I keep going through this life on earth. I said I love you out loud one final time.

I walked in the bathroom and sure enough, the candle was still lit. In one breath I blew it out. My energy shifted immediately. Instantly my body pain dissipated. I was lighter, nearly pain free. My heart was never heavier, but my body was finally able to feel and move through the stored up grief and sadness that didn't have any other way out.

I set him free, just as he did for me. As I got back in the car, the medium called me back. In all of the years she's gone through this process, never had it gone so fast. It was clear I was getting on a high speed train and this was only the beginning. I had surrendered and let go of so much to get to this point. The studio had a different feeling the next day when I went back. It was and will forever be blessed by the deepest love we can hold in this human existence. To go through this so early on was divine timing I might never understand. But one thing I know, that relationship came into my life to wake me up. The studio might not exist without it. And without either, I might still be asleep at the wheel of my own life ignoring, or deaf to, my purpose. And while yoga got me here, the practice that supported my growth, heartache and healing, I have come to realize "here" is only the beginning. Soul Dive is the foundation. It's the spark in the dark that will ignite my purposeful path forward.

A year later, around the anniversary of his death, the body pain I had experienced came back. Lo and behold, I didn't recognize it. I was falling apart, filled with overwhelming sadness and exhaustion. I practiced a lot of yoga to move it through my body and found myself in a pile of tears everytime I arrived on the mat. I did acupuncture, at which point my practitioner told me how exhausted I was by the lack of rest. I took some time to just be still in hopes I would know what was going on. In my quiet stillness the dots connected. It was early September; the anniversary of his death was a week away and the pieces started coming together. I broke down for the next two to three days. I started to feel anger rise up again. The grief, anger and sadness debilitating, physically pulling my body into dis-ease. But this time I met it all with grace. I knew the why. I knew what it was and I knew it wouldn't last forever. In fact, I was grateful I felt it.

It had been a while since I felt the presence of my fiancé. I didn't really feel him over the anniversary of his death, just the emotions swirling around our shared experience and his passing. I wasn't really allowing him to come through, if I'm honest, doing my best to try and move on romantically with my life. I didn't know how to have an ethereal relationship alongside an earthly one. Let's be honest, three's a crowd!

I wish I could tell you these emotions are linear. I wish I could say,

"Well for six months I was angry, then I was sad, then I experienced grief. Then I wrapped it all up with a pink bow and put it away on the shelf labeled 'past.'"

But that's not how it works, and my hunch is you likely know that by now. If you don't, please refer back to this when your life event hits.

The anger is what surprised me the most. I've always had a bit of a temper (thank you, Dad!) but I haven't been angry. Pure rage started to boil inside me and it continued, well into the burn period and trickled out after. Many of the emotions I was feeling then were new for me anyway. My life in Chicago was full of so much festive frivolity I wasn't feeling much. Every event I attended had a cocktail, or two, so even if the emotions were there, they were quickly numbed.

I began to realize my emotions had been wildly suppressed in August of 2019. The relationship with my fiancé had been over, and he was out of my care for nine months. I had completed my 200-

hour Yoga Teacher Training certification and hadn't quite started teaching yet. I did go to Spain for a long weekend, which as much as I love Spain and all that comes with it, didn't thrill me. I know myself well enough to go out on a limb by saying this. I wanted it all to be complete. I wanted my nine month introspective journey to have made way for the happy life I deserved to live. But there it was, anger, sitting heavily on my heart refusing to budge.

I went to Whistler, British Columbia in Canada for the Wanderlust Yoga Festival. The owner of my former home studio in Chicago brings a new teacher each year and this year she chose me. I was thrilled, and terrified that I would have to camp or something. I didn't. I was greeted with oysters and rosé in the ski village and embarked upon a beautiful journey of yoga, community, connecting with nature and a whole lot of what I now dub "good for your soul" stuff.

I won't soon forget many of the classes I took there, including Janet Stone and her One Love experience and of course Bryan Kest and his three hour mostly Warrior 3 Vinyasa practice. Those classes were amazing, but there was one that changed me. I was who I was when I walked in and who I was when I left. Donovan McGrath, who was a teacher at the Wanderlust studio in LA (which has since closed), has developed a style of yoga called Amplified Kundalini. I had never really done a Kundalini class and had no idea what to expect. I sat myself close to the front and overheard testimonials from people around me about how Donovan's classes had changed their lives. I wanted to be one of those people.

When the class began, we were invited to set an intention. Mine was simple: I didn't want to be angry anymore. I was ready to just be sad. I was ready to start mourning the life I thought I was going to have instead of going full road rage when I thought about what I didn't. I allowed myself, surrounded by 500 people, to fully drop into the experience. Jessie Blake, one of the yoga world's most notable DJs, did the music and Donovan led what was the single most physically challenging class I've ever taken. I was never in a down dog, no Warrior 2, no traditional asana poses whatsoever. The best way I can explain it is this: The anger was literally beaten out of me through the music, the movement and the magic of being surrounded by that many people. I did not walk out the same, that is for sure.

While the anger dissipated for me up on Whistler Mountain, I was still facing quite a bit of unfamiliar territory as it relates to my emotions. As much as I wanted to be normal I wasn't. I felt unrelatable, antisocial and still guilty for having fun. I hadn't come close to processing through all of the things I experienced and was experiencing; I was just wishing, hoping and praying they would go away. And they didn't.

On the heels of the anger came the sadness, self-pity and likely a hefty bout of depression. I wasn't living my purpose, I was still trying to run from the reality of my situation and cover it up with something shiny, new, tall, dark and handsome. When everything was happening nine months prior I wasn't really processing. I was simply surviving. That's what fight or flight is. We disassociate ourselves from our reality as a protection mechanism. Once it's safe to come out and re-emerge with our lives, we have to recover. I know all of this now but had no idea at the moment.

I started teaching yoga that fall. With every class I lead I felt more at home. I had been calling in so many things, like peace, purpose, and happiness, and teaching felt like I was finally moving toward my manifestations. It was late fall of 2019 when sharing the gift of yoga was really starting to feel like home. From a career perspective I knew it wouldn't be what I was going to do long term, but it felt like a really nice transition out of what I had been doing, which was running a boutique PR company for a decade. Teaching was filling up my cup. PR was not.

I have had incredible intuition for as long as I can remember. I knew that I was ready for more in my life and while I didn't know what more was, I knew I needed space for it to come in. So I started ending client contracts. Not because yoga was paying me enough to live, but because my soul needed some freedom. I needed spaciousness. I was craving change but held back by the chains of obligation, easy money and a heavy dose of complacency. But again, I made the move. One client after another. There were no hard feelings, I just needed some space.

I highly recommend this process, by the way. Faith over fear, friends. If you're calling in something more, like a career change (whether a new job or the creative space to start your own business), it's not happening if you don't have any room. Spaciousness paves the way. Allow yourself to have a break. In my case, I was still busy all the time, but teaching yoga wasn't coming home with me at night. I was making a difference in people's lives, but more than that they were making a difference in mine. Don't get me wrong, it was exhausting to hold space and teach so many classes, and I know teachers manage this all the time. But teaching was taking nowhere near the toll of doing work I was no longer passionate about.

Yoga has been the catalyst for so much in the last six years. It's hard to believe I didn't write a tribute book to the practice. This period was noteworthy because it was another risk. Saying no to contracts, which meant income, should have scared me but it didn't. What came next no one could have predicted. By March of 2020, the whole world was shutting down due to Covid. I was just ramping up my teaching when we were forced to close and go online. I will never forget the weekend in Chicago just before the shutdown. It was St. Patrick's Day weekend and if you know anything about Chicago you know the entire city lights up, the river is dyed green and the whole place is one giant party. I'm not going to lie to you. There were warnings we should stay home, and yes I heard them. But no, I didn't listen. I went out with the rest of the masses like it was one last hurrah before the shutdown. The whole town was at one big joint bachelor / bachelorette party and I wasn't going to be left behind. I topped it off with a cocktail at Soho House and a bomb dinner at Avec. I have no regrets.

Covid had some interesting timing for me. I had already been home for the better part of eighteen months and it seemed just as the world was turning in I was about ready to go out. I happily surrendered to many things, releasing FOMO for one. No one was out and I wasn't missing a thing. I could rest. I could say no. I was starting to learn how to be alone. I needed it, and quite frankly in many ways the world did too. Against all the odds and regulations, the biggest thing that emerged for me during this time was community. It took me nearly seventeen years in Chicago to fully root in a group of friends, most of whom I still consider family. It seemed like just as I was getting comfortable with a life in Chicago that I had craved for years, it was being ripped out of my fingertips. So I let it go. I let the western winds blow me out to California and I trusted the process of starting over—pandemic and all.

Here's the thing about moving across the country. You can run, but you can't hide. Some of us need to live it to learn it. All of my emotional stuff, all of the things that haunted me from caretaking, a broken relationship, a dissolved future and everything in between got packed up in the moving boxes and shipped out west. It didn't have to. I certainly could have doubled down on my work and ensured it stayed behind, but I didn't know. So off we went. I took a couple pieces of furniture, an edited wardrobe, all my Christmas decorations, and enough emotional baggage to last a lifetime.

Like I've said, grief, sadness, loss and so many emotional responses to major life events are not linear. We go through life, things happen and if you're like me, you feel it. All of it. We get cracked open so many times, not because we're meant to suffer but because we need to experience an opening to receive a greater capacity to love. The heart needs a spiritual workout; think of it like a cardio burst. Over and over, we feel. Then we have a choice. We can ignore it, close down our hearts and go numb. Or we can crack open and surrender, allowing feelings to flood our lives with what's real. It is this very transaction that brings us to the present.

After I came out on the other side of the grief following the anniversary my fiancé's death I was entering a very busy season for my new yoga business. Whether or not I was open to another visit from my fiancé is unclear. What is clear is I barely had space to shower, let alone for my soul to go on another date. But we did have another encounter. It was the end of October, 2023, a year and six weeks after he passed.

I attended a retreat in Santa Fe, New Mexico and experienced exponential growth in my heart and my business, not to mention the soulful work I didn't even know I needed. I wasn't entirely sure what I had signed up for, I just knew I had to go, get in the room and experience what was waiting for me there. What waited for me exceeded anything I could have hoped for. I transcended through quantum leaps personally and my soulful purpose ahead.

We had daily yoga, lectures, connection, sharing, time in nature, excursions, beautiful meals and all the things you'd expect on a high end retreat. On the third day we were in a breath work class. I'm no stranger to the process. When you over oxygenate the body, the pineal gland in the brain is activated, which is the same place that's activated when you take a hallucinogenic. Breath work, in my world, is also lovingly referred to as spiritual crossfit. I dropped in right away and was met with profound and prophetic visions.

First, I was standing on a stage holding this book. Keep in mind, at the time of this retreat I had not yet started writing one single page. I had pages upon pages from the years of writing and manifesting this book, but hadn't officially started. I was looking out at a crowd of thousands. My parents sat in the front row. To my right, a man was holding our baby girl. I know what I was wearing and I know what I looked like. The time was now, not in the future.

The second, I was laying down and felt a masculine presence over me, protecting me. It was him, my former fiancé. I hadn't been with him since he was in the studio after his passing. I looked at his face, happy and peaceful. The smirk across his lips was a look I saw daily when we were together. He was holding a coffee, smiling down on me, nodding his head in some kind of loving approval. Like he knew everything about my life, what I've built and the relationship I've been calling in. I felt a masculine presence move behind me, holding me like I was laying in his lap. My fiancé was above me, and my future husband sat behind me. I realized I was there to connect them and in that moment, their souls met. It was the dinner table that wasn't going to be possible this side of glory and I was holding the space for this inter-realm connection. I have secretly wished my fiancé could see me being cared for and I never thought it could be possible. But it was, and it will be once my future husband arrives in my life. The scene shifted a bit and I realized I was in labor. I had a conscious thought in this process that if I dropped into this breath pattern I could easily deliver a child (I pocketed this one for future use). As I was delivering the baby, my fiancé watched from above. When the baby arrived they knew each other—the baby and fiancé. I wasn't surprised. We all took in the moment and when it felt complete I invited my fiancé to move on. He did so graciously, lovingly, committing to always love and protect me and my future family.

I took quite a bit of time after this experience to process it. I journaled and sat in quiet stillness just being with the visions and feelings. They were real. I quite literally left the building, had them and returned back to my physical body. I was exhausted, as if I had traveled through another realm and come back in two hours.

I share this with you not to put my name on the waiting list for a bougie insane asylum. Nor do I wish to shock and awe my family or disrespect the family of my fiancé. I share it for this reason: Our whole lives exist in divine perfection. Read that again. Our hearts know what we want, what we are destined for, what our purpose here on earth looks like. Our minds block it. Our minds tell us what we should do and start comparing our experience to everyone else's. The mind might be the most fascinating part of our human bodies. My fiancé had a brilliant mind under attack by disease and I watched as Western medicine failed to save him. While we can "Oo!" and "Ahh!" over it, I believe the mind is the most corrupt and dysfunctional member of ourselves. Our minds override our intuition, causing chaos and closure to our hearts. If we only had a practice to discipline our minds and live from our hearts… imagine the peace, presence and purpose on the other side of that reality.

Chapter 12
Obligation Propaganda

"No." is a complete sentence.

In December of 2018 my dad decided to take the entire family to Italy for Christmas. It was a fully paid-for vacation in a beautiful villa and everyone would fly over firstclass. What could possibly go wrong? (Outside of just about everything.) That trip, I learned one life changing lesson that I will never again compromise: I refuse to live another day out of obligation. I'm not here to placate anyone at the expense of my own soul. I'm not here for someone else's happiness and I don't have to say yes just because it is expected that I go.

"No." is a complete sentence. One more time...

"No." is a complete sentence.

This was a brutally hard lesson for me, and one that I've had to recommit to often. It's not easy saying no, especially when the thing you're saying no to is the lap of luxury in the middle of Tuscan wine country.

I went on the trip. It was a disaster. Two out of the four of my parents' grandkids (my niece and nephew) came back and went to rehab and my mother wouldn't speak to me for months. On a positive note, my sister and I repaired a very fractured relationship. The trip came in December 2018, two months after my fiancé went back to Southern California to live with his family. I was broken, and my heart and soul were in pieces.

Thanksgiving had been just a few weeks earlier. I was supposed to fly to Palm Springs to see my parents, but Alfie had an issue and we couldn't travel. My little creature has grounded me from an airplane more than once. Each and every time it is so purposeful. So my parents pivoted at the last minute and came to Chicago. Nothing we did felt like a holiday.

We spent the weekend packing up my house as if my fiancé had died. We boxed up every piece of clothing, and sent his furniture and personal belongings back to his family or placed it in storage. It was a surreal experience and completely unfair any of us had to go through it, my parents especially. The weekend was heavy. I wasn't okay, but I lacked the ability to communicate that in any capacity. There were so many times throughout this journey where I said goodbye to him. It made me wonder if it would have been easier to just lose him in a car accident. Gone in a flash, no lingering or wondering what will happen next.

December brought more darkness to my life. I was falling apart bit by bit. I felt too much sadness to go out, but I could barely tolerate my own company to stay in. The guilt and shame of it all weighed me down with every passing day. Christmas was approaching and so was this elaborate trip to Tuscany with the whole family. My parents are insanely generous people. My dad was elated to get this house and beyond excited to share a place he loves dearly with our family. The intentions around the trip from both of my parents were nothing but pure and good. I just couldn't bring myself even close to the appreciation or excitement that should have been present for a trip like this.

I remember when my resistance started popping up. My body wasn't moving in the direction of going. I didn't pack, get organized or anything that usually takes place a week or so before leaving town. In short, I didn't want to go. I called my parents weeks before the departure date and begged them to reschedule. I pleaded that we just stay home. Have a quiet holiday alone, just the three of us. I was desperate for comfort, familiarity, and solace. I wanted a familiar space to just be. I didn't even know how to identify my feelings at the time; I just knew I was falling apart. I was told to take it or leave it. They couldn't make me get on the plane, but if I didn't I was going to spend Christmas alone. Their response lacked empathy or understanding. Neither could relate to what I was experiencing. I later learned Brené Brown's definition of empathy and will forever hold this one close to my heart. She defines it as "relating to the emotion underpinning the experience, not the experience itself." To them at that time, it was nothing more than another breakup. To me, it was so much more.

I walked into Terminal 5 at O'Hare in tears. I sobbed the entire Uber ride to the airport. I didn't want to be there. It was the expectation that drove the obligation to show up. Even in hindsight a big part of me wishes I leaned into my internal knowing that I didn't want to go— that gut feeling to stay home and just be with myself; even in the sadness and unimaginable loneliness that would have come with that particular Christmas. But I didn't. I went and stepped into obligation, which in this case was the lion's den of unhealed emotional drama.

Everyones got their stuff, this I know. But this was like stuff on steroids. When I arrived at the airport, I was greeted by my mother on the phone with my fiancé begging him to come join us. It was as if resurrecting him and our relationship, or ignoring the reality of his situation, was going to make this all better. Next my nephew dumped his latest update on me: He had gotten kicked out of college and wanted my sympathy. Um, pass, thank you.

It was one of the messiest weeks I've ever experienced. It lacked any amount of joy and my emotional capacity to relish in the company of family was too thin to bear. The events that transpired during the week we were all supposed to be living our best Diane Lane lives *Under the Tuscan Sun* were not suited for my post trauma reality. Some might say this was normal family drama. And that's fine, I've come to accept the dynamic of a blended family is complicated and cluttered with old stories, history and a hefty amount of baggage. But because I accept it, that doesn't mean I have to sign up for it. Just because I have a blood connection to the players doesn't mean I need to be a part of the game. Can we normalize getting on the bench here? We do not have to show up just because it's family. We also don't have to make it an all or nothing deal—Like I'm skipping Christmas and the rest of life together. No, we can simply sit things out here and there in an effort to *pre-serve* the self. Yes, pre serve, if you break down the word preserve this is what that means. We take care of ourselves so we can show up whole. Doing so plants grace at the center of our heart. Not doing so is a slippery slope to soulsucking disaster.

I left Italy grateful for my sister. Our relationship was always a bit out of balance and historically quite challenging. The trip, and all the chaos that ensued, forced us to communicate. We spent much of our time there together. We day tripped to Montalcino and shipped incredible wine home; this is at the top of my best travel memories. On our last night, she shared something with me that has weighed heavily on her heart for decades. Over dinner and our last bottle of Italian red, she said this:

I got the dad she never did.

Her words landed powerfully on my heart. I knew she was right. It was no one's fault, simply what is.

We have the same dad, but different moms. She was twenty-one when I was born. My dad was forty-two when he became my father and was in a different place in his life when he had my sister during his first marriage. Hearing her echo the truth without assumption, blame, or resentment was beautiful. She was right. She spoke from a heart-centered place and it changed the trajectory of our relationship. Her share came free of blame; I got a different version of my dad. The moment her words left her mouth our relationship became lighter. Those feelings held no power over her anymore. They were out in the open, fresh air dissipated any previous weight once held by an old story, pent up emotion and the longing for freedom.

This trip showed me a lot of things I may or may not have been ready for at the time. But the biggest lesson I took away from the whole experience is this: living in obligation keeps you from experiencing freedom. When we show up for what we have to do because someone else expects us to do it, we aren't aligned with showing up for ourselves. At the end of the day it really all comes down to freedom. In hindsight, I'm grateful I got on the plane. Obligatory living is a difficult pattern to break and this one cracked through to the epicenter for me putting a big period at the end of the word no when it comes to something that isn't a full body yes.

If you ask me what I think most people actually want in life I'm going to tell you freedom. If you would have asked me what I wanted years ago I would have rattled off a bunch of things, freedom not being one of them. When we're told we have it, we often don't think about wanting it, needing it or asking for it. Freedom comes in many forms. It can be financial, time or connections. When we are young, sure, there are rules. We enter the sandbox of childhood with some boundaries but we're actually quite free. We create, invent, use our voices and show kindness to strangers. We aren't living in fear, worry or doubt. We're kept safe by the confines of our proverbial playpens and our souls experience the sense of wonder and freedom that come with having little to nothing to worry about. We take it for granted, forget how much we loved it and only when we arrive as adults, oftentimes prisoners in our own bodies, do we come to realize it's likely the single most important thing we can have.

As it turns out, freedom is one of the things I want most in life. My dad has been telling me this about myself for years.

It's freedom you crave.

Good for you, creating a life where you have all the freedom.

I cringed when I heard it years ago in the throws of owning my consulting business. I wanted to be recognized for how many clients I had, the high profile events I produced and attended, and the income I was generating. I failed to recognize what I actually built was a life full of freedom. I set my own hours, traveled frequently, booked any appointment I wanted in the middle of the day, left my desk for yoga on the regular, and went out any night of the week if I wanted to. I was free, no golden handcuffs, no governing body, just me.

Reflecting back, I was in my late twenties when I started running. At first it was simply an activity to catch up with two dear friends that were avid runners. We were growing out of the daily drinking phase so in an effort to make a healthier choice, I told them I'd run until they went too far for me to hang. I completed an eighteen mile run and snagged a last-minute bib to run the Bank of America Chicago Marathon fundraising for the Lincoln Park Zoo. Go big or go home I suppose. It's really not in my nature to do a half marathon because why on earth would I want to turn around and do the whole thing again? Just go for it. And! Pro tip: run for the zoo and you can use their bathrooms around mile four. Game changer, and no porta potty was required for my race! I also finished with mascara still intact so you do the math as to how swiftly I was moving.

When I think about why I signed up for the race in the first place, the answer was around discipline. I had all this freedom, which while I didn't know how to name, I was acutely aware I had it. I wondered if I could actually hold myself to a training routine which would allow me to safely and happily complete the race. I did and to this day I'll tell you it was one of the best days of my adult life. I had friends every two miles. My parents showed up at multiple points and at the half, brought Alfie down for a little visit. My crew was in utter disbelief that I would do it. I not only did it, but booked a blowout at my apartment after curling up in bed for a couple hours to recover before drinking champagne and eating chicken fingers at the bar downstairs. Claim it! Nothing beats an expensive bottle of bubbly with a fresh batch of chicken fingers. Amen!

My dad was right, as he often is. I was indeed quite free. I would run my business for a month in Europe, never missing a beat. To this day I haven't celebrated the beautiful business I created that was so rooted in freedom. How could I have not realized it? I was a bit foolish and unaware of what I had. There are times I reflect back to that part of my life and think I would give almost anything to go back. That's the lovely thing about how destructive our minds can be when thoughts are produced. They lack all the details, creating a false reality and push us into the *grass is always greener* mindset when we let our thoughts wander too far without discipline. It is quite easy for me to think,

Oh it was better back then.

But it wasn't. The truth is I wasn't living in my truth. My naivete had some perks, yes, and working from the south of Spain happened to be one of them. But I wasn't rooted in my purpose and I wasn't palpably happy. I had a taste of freedom, but it wasn't an embodiment of who I am. That's the place I'm stepping into now: full of purpose, embodiment of freedom.

My craving for freedom didn't just start in my early thirties from some beach in Spain. I've been living this way since I was a child. When I was a kid my mom would force me to take piano lessons. I could play anything by ear. Little humble brag here, but it really is a gift to be able to do this. I learned to play the piano before I learned how to read. The teachers didn't want to confuse me (thanks for the vote of confidence, guys) so I was not taught how to read music right away. I loved it. It was a little taste of freedom, maybe along the lines of cooking with no recipe. Everything to taste. The rub came when my mom would harp on me to practice. I didn't like being told what to do. I still don't. She would tell me to play, I would refuse. This was one of many domestic wars that would transpire in our house.

I remember being old enough to stay home alone while my parents would go out. I would watch the car leave and head straight to the piano. I would play all the songs I loved, my favorite being Beauty and the Beast (or "Tale as Old as Time") from the soundtrack of the Disney classic, *Beauty and the Beast*. When I saw the car come back down the street I would get up and run upstairs. I never admitted liking to play and certainly never told them I would only practice if allowed to do so on my own terms and timing. I can feel the eyes roll from here, trust me.

I never thought to place freedom on my list of desires because I was told I already had it. After all, I live in America, the land of the free, home of the brave! But here's a hard truth: freedom is not inherited. And another hard truth: Happiness can, in part, be bought. We cultivate freedom through devotional practices and hard work. We have to set ourselves up to achieve it and stay in the flow to maintain it. Freedom might in fact be our birth right, but it's not guaranteed, not inherent, not a given and absolutely not always easy to achieve. I would go so far as to say the antithesis of freedom is obligation. When we live for our obligations, the shoulds, expectations, and self or third party imposed demands, we are stripping ourselves of the ability to actually be free. That's exactly what I had done. I was raised by the obligatory propaganda and lived "freely" and quite lavishly behind the bars of expectations.

There is an argument to be made for obligation. I can hear the baby boomers chirping from here.

"You have to work, make a living and provide for yourself."

They promote the grind, the hustle, and the American dream! There's truth and toxicity in those messages, neither right or wrong. I am the first to admit that we must work hard to financially take care of ourselves. But I'll take it a step further. You fall into obligation when you're too lazy and complacent to drop into purpose. Just having a job isn't good enough, in my opinion. Each and every part of your life provides an opportunity to embody passion, purpose and presence. You get to choose it. Why are you hating it every step of the way? It's up to you to grow, do the work and create a life that you deem worth living—a life that frees your mind and your soul. If you're embodying the work, not just your nine to five but the real work, you will undoubtedly reap the reward by feeling a true sense of lightness, happiness and freedom.

Obligations are driven by expectations. We all fall victim to this and I can't say it loud enough. If it's not a full body yes, it's a hard no. I arrived here after years doing and living as I should, by other people's opinions and expectations. I never fully understood I didn't have to. My obligations were what some would say excellent problems to have. My mother could spend all day in Neiman Marcus, whereas I start to feel like a caged animal if I was there for more than an hour. Was I forced to stay? Not really. But I was taught that it's important to spend time with family. I was well into my thirties before I realized I could use my voice to influence where the family bonding could happen. I'm also proud to report we've found other ways to spend time together. I guess this is what living with your parents for four years will do for you!

I lived most of my life in obligation and expectation, one of the biggest drivers being my parents and the conversion around family. To them, my mother in particular, we are obligated to spend time with family because, well, they are family. Without giving you a script that could put the Kardashians out of business, I'll simply say this. My family, like most, has a complicated dynamic. I have three half siblings, all now married (some multiple times and let's just say you can't choose who someone else marries) and four nieces and nephews. The dynamics are complex, loaded with emotions like resentment, envy, greed and competition. Over and over my parents have tried to get the whole crew together and each time it goes up in smoke. They forget, and the pattern repeats.

What breaks the pattern and therefore tears down the walls of obligation is choice. Choice implies and inspires freedom. When we choose to say yes to something that feels so right in our whole body, we are showing up because we actually want to. I firmly believe that the body knows whether or not we really want to do something. We might think we do want something, but if we haven't moved in the direction required to make it happen I would question whether it's a full body yes or agreeing out of obligation.

Obligation is soulsucking. Obligation breeds resentment like a wildfire. Obligation is people pleasing and being a doormat. It's stuff that drives me absolutely nuts. We are human beings with free will. We aren't obligated to do anything. If you're reading this, triggered by my definitions of freedom and counting the oh-so-many ways you are obligated to show up in your life, check yourself, honey. What if we *get* to do all the things we do instead of *having* to do them? Could we reshape the narrative and fall in love with saying yes because we mean it?

When I fully realized most of my life was lived out of obligation I got really comfortable saying no, really fast. Saying no and not offering a reason will piss many people in your life off. Big time. Saying no because you don't want to. Saying no because you choose you. It's bold, but essential if you're living your truth. I stepped into my voice of yes or no and the first person triggered was my mother. We're not talking big stuff here, at least not to me. But I started to lean into what I actually wanted to do. When invited to shop I said I would meet later so I could take a yoga class first. When I would visit my parents in California I would leave the house for the day to go on a long hike up in the mountains. To which my mom actually responded,

"Why?"

Because my soul needs to be outside. My body needs to move. I need to breathe fresh air. I'm also happy to report she's getting it now and even, occasionally, gets herself on a yoga mat. Baby steps are still steps.

When I started shifting out of obligation, choosing myself and the things that give me life, I started to experience some resistance. Friendships and relationships began falling by the wayside. My priorities changed, as did how I wanted to spend my time. I noticed my mom's resistance to my no's. My mom didn't have the life I had growing up. She got married for the first time extremely young and had my brother when she was nineteen years old. She was hard working, and after divorcing her first husband a couple years later, proved she could single-mother it like the best of them. Her life was full of love, family, friends and a respectable career. Her life was also chock-full of obligation. She didn't, and still doesn't, experience the type of freedom I'm talking about. I hear it all the time, the things she "has" to do. She actually doesn't "have" to do anything; she's choosing to be held hostage by the old stories and obligatory dialogue of shoulds. The invitation still stands to break free, and I dare you (and her!) to accept it.

My mother has always been a big part of my life, witnessing me flourish and travel, living unattached and full of freedom. The older I got, the more I learned how to choose myself by selecting the things that filled me up. Department store? Not so much. Eating out at restaurants? Nope. Time outside? Yes. Cooking clean food? Hell yes. I started protecting my time and energy a bit more, becoming less and less likely to agree to something that didn't feel fully aligned.

My mom brought me into the world when she was thirty-seven and has been living for me ever since. When I was younger I would tell her to get a life and get a job. That's such an asshole thing to say. I think what I meant was go find something you're passionate about and allow your soul to get filled up by doing it—get excited about something. Choose the thing that brings you joy. Stretch your mind, move your body, learn something or connect with different people. I didn't have the right words as a (at times) snotty teenager. I watched my mom take care of everyone else because she thought she had to. She was, and still is, always the first one someone calls when they need something. She falls victim to other people's bullshit and it physically takes a toll on her. I've witnessed the breakdowns. I watched her take care of my grandmother, putting outfits and jewelry together so that she could get dressed with dignity each day in the nursing home, ready for the happy hour gin and tonic every afternoon at 4:00 p.m.

I watched, and still watch, my mom take on the burdens and baggage of friends and loved ones because she cares. The problem is she can't release it. She carries it, places it in her own heavy bags and allows the weight of things that aren't even hers to begin with, to pull her down. I've witnessed her come down with everything from the stomach flu to body pain as a result. Mom, if you're reading this, it's never too late to learn how to take off the handcuffs of obligation and step into the air of freedom.

I've seen glimpses of it, my mom embodying the freedom I hope she believes she deserves. Most recently on an unforgettable trip to the South of France. I flew out ahead of time and spent a few days on my own in a little Italian town called Bordighera followed by a couple days in Cannes. I picked her up at the Nice airport and our first stop was the Hotel De Paris in Monte-Carlo, Monaco. The property is across the square from the famed casino. A surreal experience. From the mega yachts down at the harbor to droves of tourists who watch people who are also on vacation, being on vacation, Monaco is one of those places that feels more like a James Bond movie set than a real place. We dined at the hotel our first night, mesmerized by the the whole scene. The table next to ours sat three Americans and one Brit, all from Newport Beach. As fate would have it, my mom's future spinal surgeon was among the group. Go ahead, tell me God didn't have his hands all over this one...

I discovered a little beach town about 15 minutes away called Saint-Jean-Cap-Ferrat. I fell in love with the quaint marina and to this day can envision a Soul Dive Yoga sitting peacefully next to the little shop that outfitted me for the rest of my trip in the South of France. I took my mom back to the area for lunch on our way to Saint

Tropez. Each place we went more beautiful than the last. We arrived in Saint Tropez just before dinner. At first blush it was a charming Mediterranean beach town. Cobblestone streets, beautiful shops, cafes and of course, the port donning the most miraculous yachts (a close second to the mega status up in Monaco). We spent the next four days in heaven. We shopped, went to the beach clubs, dinned at some of the best restaurants and met lovely people along the way. You'd think is was like any other European holiday… until our last day.

We had a lunch reservation at Lulu Ramatuelle. The beach clubs open about 10am and you can choose whether or not you'd like the early seating at noon, later seating around 2:00 or 3:00pm or simply enjoy the offerings from your Gucci-clad beach chairs gazing out at the Mediterranean Sea. We made friends with a sweet couple from Switzerland, sitting next to us on the beach. They invited us to join them for lunch at the club next door, Le Palmiers. We accepted and quickly learned that La Palmiers was under the same ownership as L'Opera, of which we had just enjoyed the late (or festive) seating for dinner the night before. The lunch was beautiful, fantastic food, incredible champagne. As the meal comes to a close, the waitstaff clear all of the plates and get the tables ready. One by one patrons start taking to the table to dance. Everyone in the place was beautiful, impeccably dressed and happy.

I left for a moment to take a dip in the water and upon my return, a man and a woman were taking my mom's hand and hoisting her up on their table. I couldn't get there fast enough to stop it, and when I did arrive I was whisked up to join her. There is a video that will live on my Instagram grid forever documenting the event. My mom was Saint Tropez royalty. Her outfit was a 10, her glasses perfection and the cowboy hat she had purchased the day before was the cherry on top. She looked dynamite. What's more, she had the time of her life. The Queen of Saint Tropez I called her for months following the trip. I watched my 75 year-old mother live with such unbridled joy and unmatched freedom. We walked for miles around town, danced on tables with beautiful Europeans by day and stayed out until all hours by night. We shopped, ate the local Tart Tropezien and went crazy at the outdoor flea market that happens weekly. To say this is my favorite place on earth would be an understatement. I discovered that while I feel an affinity to Spain and a deep love for Italy, I'm a Francophile at heart. The French are proper, kind and have unmatch style and sophistication. I could go on about my love affair with France, especially the South of France. But what was so remarkable about this experience was seeing my mother in what felt like her natural habitat. My mom is from small town Iowa, not even Des Moines (which is in some circles considered the Paris of the Prairie). She couldn't have been raised in an environment more different from Saint Tropez. But yet, watching her saunter down the streets of the old city, indulge in late-night fine dining and the dance party to end all dance parties, I can't help but wonder if her soul has been there, or has always hailed from there, time and time again. Watching her embody a sense of freedom I've rarely seen in my 38 years of life was the greatest gift.

Sharing the experience with my mom in the South of France gave me the validation I knew all along. She has all the makings for a life that embodies freedom. Most of us do, but a mindset rooted in obligation keeps us stuck. Sometimes we choose to remain in the hostage situation because it's all we know. Dipping the toe outside into the unknown is scary, maybe even uncomfortable at first. True freedom exists outside of any confines. When you arrive it feels unknown, like a foreigner landing in a new country, language barrier and all. Freedom is living wholeheartedly heart centered. The governance no longer comes from the outside, but rather from within.

The freedom land is at your fingertips but could feel like worlds (and lifetimes) away. Reaching it is, and the work is rooted in surrender. Freedom is achieved only when we release the grip and allow for what is supposed to be, to actually be. It's letting go of control and judgements and flowing with those unexpected things life sometimes places abruptly on our lap. Freedom is listening to the voice in your heart that knows and disciplining the voices in your head that don't.

I watch people live in obligation all the time. You should hear the resistance that comes my way from those I invite in for yoga.

"I don't have time."

"I'm not flexible."

"I've got dinner plans."

Oh the list goes on and on. The chains of obligatory living are so tight we can't even see a good thing when it's placed right in front of our nose. When we default to the comfortable, we start living in complacency. Complacency is evil. I can't stand it and it makes me physically ill to witness how widespread this lazy approach to life is for so many people.

You are given a beautiful world to explore, create, connect and thrive in. And you're choosing to remain comfortable in stagnation because you're too afraid to say yes to what your heart really desires. Trust me, your heart doesn't desire the million loads of laundry or mediocre dinner plans. Your heart doesn't desire the partner you settled with because you doubted the right man is out there. Your heart doesn't want to have dinner with your creepy uncle just because he is family. Your heart doesn't want the job, your heart wants the full embodied yes of a thriving career. Your heart wants to be loved, respected, nourished and kept safe. Anything that falls outside of these bounds is not for you. And if it's not for you it will fall away from you. Obligation is a slippery slope, my friends. Most likely, if you say yes and it's not your purpose you'll get a divine redirect, or worse, your own 2x4 moment that knocks you on your ass.

We get so used to defaulting into *yes* that *no* feels like a swear word when it exits our lips. Obligation leads to stagnant, complacent energy. It's what gets you stuck and once stuck, it's a heck of a lot harder to get unstuck. Obligation will take a piece of your soul. If this makes you uncomfortable I invite you into the work. Consider this your invitation to surrender and release. Allow parts of your life to burn to the ground to make room for spaciousness. Will you accept it? Will you finally say yes to creating space for what your heart desires instead of living for someone else's expectations? Once you do, and make a commitment to live authentically through your heart, you will experience the intoxicating rise of being fully you. You are enough, you are worth working for and you are worthy of having each and every single thing your heart desires. You just have to believe it, claim it and step into it.

Chapter 13
Soulful Alchemy: Rising from the Ashes

Starting over is a soulful act of bravery.

I was sitting at dinner with my new and very dear friend PJ at the beach a couple months before this book came into the world. He knows my story and from time to time, asks questions that take me back to the days I was with my fiancé. Last night was one of those times. We were talking about my dating life (a subject that seems to breed content for days) and I was sharing something that has never left my heart. I was blessed to have already experienced the greatest love. The kind of love you watch in the movies. The love at first sight, "when you know you know" kind of love. I received unconditional love from a man that would have done anything to make me happy. We were struck by tragedy and in our case, never got to live out the fairytale I have been dreaming about since I was a kid. But I've had it and as painful as it was to lose it, I fall into the cliché that it is better to have loved and lost than to have never loved at all.

The point I was making to PJ is maybe my quest for love could look different this time. Maybe I don't need the great love that defies the odds and is made for romance novels. Maybe I just need a nice man to raise a family with and live simply. Love, sure. But maybe I don't need the Big Love.

PJ has a mohawk, and after my fiancé was done with his chemo and radiation treatment, he lost most of his hair and rocked a mohawk as well. For some reason on this night I was reminded of him, my fiancé, and was sharing more than usual with PJ about our love. He needed a visual so I pulled up some old photos. He zoomed in on a moment from our engagement party. We paused, nothing needed to be said and within seconds PJ was in tears, sweetly crying into his wine glass. He looked at me and said in no uncertain terms: You will have this again. You deserve to have this again. He's out there, you just have to believe that.

I have spent years of my adult life in some kind of isolation. Being a business owner is quite isolating. Going through trauma, isolating. Healing, for me, was isolating. Moving to California, isolating. Going back and forth between the beach and the desert, isolating. This theme has been with me for a while and thanks to my awareness, the time finally arrived to break the pattern. I kept finding myself on the bench of my own life, working on myself or my business, and not living in it. I was doing all of the fussing around, hurrying up so I could make more time and space to relax, enjoy, travel and just be. But it wasn't happening. I kept myself isolated in the hustle, grind and perfection. It. Was. Exhausting.

We are not meant to do this—any of this—alone. We are meant to be in community, in divine union and partnership with others.

Isolation is the devil's work, if you ask me. It's where we fall victim to our fears, anxieties and worries. Isolation is not synonymous with solitude. We can be around people and still feel very isolated. Just like we can even be in a romantic relationship and feel lonely (which is a space I've also been in).

I share this anecdote, sitting at dinner tears pouring into our wine glasses, because I need you to know a few things. No matter how much healing work you do around grief, loss or trauma, the pain is still there and your emotions are very real. We spent a good fifteen minutes in tears. I told PJ how much he would have loved my fiancé. He could tell. He's been less than impressed by the lot of men that have come through my life and his tears were both happy I had it and sad I lost it.

The moment also solidifies this very simple truth: You do not need to be fully healed to be completely loved. Putting yourself on the bench, taking yourself out of your life is choosing isolation. There is never a scenario where you can fully recover and heal, then get back out there as a perfectly healed human. It's not possible. The way we heal and grow is through connection. We can absolutely spend time alone in prayer, reflection and meditation—those are powerful practices. But it is through others, the community and connection, as a collective we all rise.

The moment with PJ and our tearstained wine glasses reminded me that our deadlines are arbitrary. If I could have disappeared into the abyss to re-emerge as a fully healed version of myself I would have done it by now. It is a process, a constantly evolving journey. It has required a hefty amount of grace and a heart full of faith. No matter how challenging, I'm also constantly reminded that we can always start over. Life, for the most part, is full of opportunities to begin again.

Second chances, new beginnings and fresh starts are at the tips of our fingers. We just have to be brave enough to accept them.

Starting over is a soulful act of bravery.

Starting over implies we're entering a space we've never been. Uncharted territory with no rulebook. It's uncertain and we're invited to get comfortable with that. Starting over is no easy task, the older we get the more rooted, programmed and stuck in what we know, it becomes nearly impossible to slide into something new. We are invited to start over all the time. With each new experience we take what we learned, apply it to the path forward and release what doesn't serve us on our journey ahead. Take what you love, leave what you don't. Sound familiar? It's not new information and is rooted in one very important concept: Choice.

The choice is yours to continue living the life you're used to, or accept the invitation to grow. Growth is the path to the life you were put here on this earth to live. You have a choice: Evolve or remain stagnant. Embody the life you're given, or remain a passive puppet to the expectations and obligations placed on you by others. No one out there is going to do it for you, friends. It is completely and entirely up to you. It is your job to become aware you're out of alignment, make a conscious effort to shift, and surrender into the process it takes to come out on the other side. You are not only responsible for learning, but you're responsible for applying the lessons. That's wisdom. Be wise.

Life has a beautiful way of preparing us for what's next. We're introduced to people, places and tiny divine moments all the time. Even when we're not paying attention the plan is playing out, in our favor if we let it. Each encounter is more purposeful than the last, and each redirect harnesses greater potential to infuse more love, purpose and presence into our existence. I firmly believe this. I believe we are invited into scenarios and scenes our minds can't comprehend because it's for us, and not working against us. I believe wholeheartedly we don't have to, nor are we going to, like each and every scene we get to play in. Much of life can be gut wrenchingly awful; it makes getting out of bed feel impossible.

To the contrary, the magnificence of human existence never ceases to amaze me. From our intuitive knowing to our innate resilience, being human comes with all forms of tragedy and triumph, grit and grace, force and surrender, strength and ease. We are guided into opportunities to learn, apply information and evolve. It's a choice. Resisting growth offers you a one way ticket to death, by way of stagnation, complacency and boredom. Saying yes offers you the trip of a lifetime.

I lived most of my adult life asleep at the wheel. Everything was fine. Things looked beautiful and depending on who you asked, my life was pretty darn enviable. I didn't know much but seemed to gain a lot. I floated through my early adult years with a beautifully painted façade. I could have kept going down the familiar rabbit hole logging more and more years in Chicago doing the same things with the same people over and over again, my beautiful yet mediocre existence playing on one continuous loop. It happens to all of us. We suddenly arrive somewhere and wonder,

"How the heck did I get here?"

We notice a part of ourselves is lost, or we become shockingly aware that we don't know the soul occupying our human suit. Either way, back to choice.

I made the choice to get off the complacent merry go round and buckled down on bravery. It took a lot to wake me up, and when it was all happening I knew one day I would be grateful for it. The day has arrived where I no longer curse the experience that played out on my 33rd birthday. I'm immensely grateful for it. I am grateful for each moment of hurt, pain and suffering. I'm grateful for the love I shared with my fiancé because it taught me more in nine months than some people allow themselves to learn in a lifetime. The tragic events laid the foundation for me to either rise up, or fall by the wayside. There was no middle ground. Sink or swim, live or die. I was put on the edge of a cliff with a glimmer of knowing in my heart that said you're meant for more. I was placed beside the ocean and heard Jesus call me into the deep not knowing what that meant or where I would go. I was told to have faith and fly because standing still would crumble me to death. So I did it.

I remember waking up on June 16, 2023, the morning of my 38th birthday. Something felt different. I took my journal out in the sunshine and spent two hours in free flowing, stream of consciousness. I was lighter. Physically, emotionally and spiritually lighter. It dawned on me that my life was no longer on fire. That the phase where everything I knew, attached to and identified with was already gone and I was left with just me. Sitting in that moment was some of the best news I've received in my entire life. My world was set on fire in 2018 and in 2023 it stopped. Five full years of burning to the ground. The old stories, patterns, people, etc. all went up in smoke. The release is a powerful moment, especially when you realize it has happened. When I think back on it I have to laugh a little. You'd think after five years on fire all the baggage was already burned to the ground, but low and behold, the work to let go is never done.

As I moved through this period, forced to let go (and gripping so tightly at first) I eventually landed in the sweet space of surrender. That was my word of the year in 2022, the year Soul Dive Yoga came to be. I struggled for a bit with the undeniable polarity between surrender and hustle. I have always hustled, created, built, sustained, and all the other power words associated with being a business owner. Surrender wasn't part of the dialogue until now. Surrender became the new hustle and I can assure you, I work overtime at letting go and allowing. Allowing is one of the hardest things we can do as humans, especially when we're asked to allow something uncomfortable to unfold. But we have to allow, and trust that it's supposed to be that way. And we have to know that because we are rooted in faith. When we are rooted in faith, we can rest without fear knowing God has his hands placed right over our hearts.

What has become abundantly clear to me is that *strength* is not what I needed to get through any of the things I've experienced in my life. For me, it was never the mentality of "Just power through," "Get over it," or the classic, "Put your big girl panties on and deal with it."

This is old programming, an outdated paradigm that kept my nervous system in fight or flight for way too long. I chose to rewire my brain to accept a new approach. The path forward isn't about pushing or forcing. The path forward has invited me to soften, expand, and let surrender be the new hustle. It's been an invitation to let go and allow, and actually live by faith and not out of fear. It's also not an overnight job. Time and again I falter, finding myself back in the saddle of control pushing the agenda I want for my life, especially in times of refusing to tap into the greater knowing of what I need.

When we find ourselves in the space of control, force and agenda-pushing, there is only one way out. Start over. Throw up your white flag, take a ten breaths or a ten-minute savasana, and begin again. Get back in the sweet spot of surrender and recommit to the process of allowing life to unfold as it will—knowing it's for you and not against. Knowing you are divinely loved and protected.

I felt compelled to share my story with you because it breaks my heart to know how many people feel alone—like there is no one else that has walked in your shoes or knows how you feel. I've been there. I don't know one other 33-year-old that was caring for their terminally ill fiancé . The support that showed up around me couldn't relate, and therefore I pushed it away. I didn't know how to receive. I believe strongly in the power of community and if I can impart just one little tidbit to you it's this: You are not alone and the people that love you don't need to experience the same thing to support you. We all identify with feelings of sadness, fear, anxiety and heartbreak. Lucky us! They are guaranteed in the human experience. Bonus round, we actually get to experience these emotions over and over during our time on earth. But there's good news. We wouldn't know happiness, joy, pleasure and love without pain. There is always light, even in the darkest corners of our hearts and I'm here to tell you, the light always wins out. We wouldn't know the dark without the light so the next time your heart ends up as roadkill, find a glimmer of gratitude in knowing that you won't be there forever.

I found that the more I shared my experience the more I found people that could relate and hold even the tiniest bit of space for my pain. The healing process for anything, grief included, is not linear. Even the experiences that you have processed can creep back with an emotional response. Let them. I don't know that there will ever be a day when I look at photos of my fiancé and don't feel sad. Even when I land in my happily ever after and become one of those assholes that posts the perfect picture on Instagram and tries to convince you that my life is perfect, the pain will still be there. These experiences live in your body forever and instead of resisting or feeling guilty they're there, just allow and fall back into surrender.

I desperately wanted to end this book by telling you that I finally found Big Love again, married the man of my dreams and have the beautiful baby girl I've dreamed of. But that's just not where we're at. At the point of publication, I'm single, navigating the Southern California dating scene. While it's not the storybook version of happily ever after, I have arrived gracefully in my purpose and find nothing happier than living with peace. If this life brings me the man of my dreams, and I very much believe he is out there, I will be forever grateful. But if it doesn't, and the love I had six years ago was the one I got for this lifetime, I know in my heart and soul it was big enough to sustain this life and more.

One of the biggest realities and toughest truths I've had to accept is that we are not meant to know what's next. Biblically speaking, we are asked, tasked and challenged to trust (over and over and over this theme prevails). I hated this for years. I resisted it and forced my life to align with the outcomes I wanted so I didn't have to be in the space of not knowing. So I could always know, control and be ready. But that is not how it works, and in fact all the plotting and planning makes it that much harder to recover when you're forced to pivot— no matter how big or small the pivot might be.

As I move forward, I am comfortable not knowing exactly how things are going to play out. I think there's so much beauty in allowing divine order to be what is. It's certainly a lot less work, I can tell you that. I've experienced a lot and have quite a bit to share. But simultaneously, I don't know where to send my mail and I couldn't tell you where home is. As much as it might seem as though I've got it all figured out, I can assure you I don't. I can tell you what I want the future to look like and where I think I'm going. I can promise you I'll make moves to get there. But I really don't know with full certainty I'll arrive there, and is there really a *there* there anyway? Who knows, in the next few months—in the space between this book being in draft and debut, I could get married, move to France, launch a TedTalk or start another business. I don't know and I'm so glad I don't. Information is revealed when we're ready to receive it. Whenever I'm getting a little antsy or feel like I need a more obvious sign I ask for it. I pray, talk to the angels and light a little fire under the ethereal team supporting my earthly experience.

Conclusion

The day after I was sitting at the bar with my friend PJ, I woke up as I do most mornings. I made my bed, poured a coffee and sat myself on my couch with my journal on my left and my computer on my right. I wasn't sure what I felt like doing with the hour of downtime I had before the day needed to start. I asked for a sign and got a ping to check my bank account. One of my accounts had five nines repeating. Five! That's a record for me. The number nine represents endings and beginnings and in that moment I knew. It was time to open my computer and put a big pink bow on this book. Endings feel so final, like we can't change it if it's the end. And that does have a fair amount of truth to it. But here's the thing about this ending, which is like so many others because, well, all endings really are quite similar. The end is required to begin again. We have to say goodnight before it makes sense to say good morning. The numbers told me it was time to pen the end, put a period at the end of the last sentence and close the computer. Because without it, we just keep going and going and going and if there is one thing I've learned, we have to stop, collaborate and listen. And in those quiet moments of the early morning - and so many mornings like it - I did just that.

As all great endings begin, I will offer you this final conclusion. My story is so much more than the tragic heartbreak I experienced with my fiancé. But that tragedy was required; it was through that very ending that I got the biggest new beginning I may ever have in my life. Not all beginnings are created equally and I feel blessed beyond measure I was smacked upside the head with the 2x4 at 33 and not 83. We don't have infinite time in our earthly experience. We're only given so many breaths and like beginnings, not all endings are created equally as well. The last breath is it. There's no coming back to this space and time once we breath that last conclusive cycle. But in the space between—the liminal space that exists between this breath and your last, what are you doing? Are you living in complacency or are you brave enough to get off the bench and step into your life instead of hiding from it?

I was asked the very same day I wrote this last chapter what it was that I wanted to impart on my readers. I want you to know you're not alone. No matter how lonely or isolated you feel, you are not alone. I was asked what kept me going, during the darkest moments when I hit the very bottom of my own existence. Despite living with a compromised nervous system, in a perpetual state of fight or flight, I kept going to yoga. I went because I wasn't judged. No one knew what I was going through and I could just simply be in whatever way, shape or form I showed up. What kept me going was curiosity. Something was happening at a cellular level and it kept me coming back to my mat, time and again.

There is so much you can take away from my story. I could have faded into the abyss of complacency and partied my way well into the second half of my life. Thankfully I didn't. Thankfully I hopped in the middle of my very own dumpster fire and allowed myself to rise up from the ashes. Not fully healed, not free from guilt, shame, anxiety and sadness. But proudly wearing the emotional scars that had been placed on my heart over the years and armed with the tools and tactics to continue the pattern of getting out of bed and living in my life, not on the sidelines.

It is only when we double down on our own self love, worth and compassion that we can truly rise from the ashes, no matter what has burned beneath our fragile feet. I did it. I stepped out of the rubble and looking back, I can dust my shoulders off and remove the rose colored glasses. It's not hard to meet my own gaze anymore. On the other side of all of it—no matter what it is for you—is a freedom you might not even know exists. It's accepting the hard truths because once you've lived a certain amount of life, the happy horseshit just doesn't cut it.

Once you get comfortable with the truth, receive grace and let *surrender* be your hustle, you will live with more ease and experience far more peace. I know it. I've done it. And it's available to you as well. If you don't know where to start, just remember it's always at the beginning. Find yourself a yoga studio and take it one breath at a time. That's all we can do. In the fire, fan the flame. It's only through the burn that you will enjoy the beautiful bounty that awaits on the other side— and that other side is freedom. It's only from the ashes you can rise. It's only after the burn you can find bliss. The whole process is Soulful Alchemy. The unexplainable, ethereal, process of always leaning into love and constantly letting go. It is when, and only when, we embody that process will the rubble make way for us all to collectively rise—mind, body and soul.

Here's What To Do Next

1. Access All Your Free Bonuses

Visit www.soulfulalchemist.com to access FREE resources and bonus content.

2. Visit Soul Dive Yoga

Join Alex in Palm Desert for a class at Soul Dive Yoga! Visit www.souldiveyoga.com for more information and to book a class.

3. Hire Alex To Speak

For more information about hiring Alex for speaking engagements, private events and retreats visit www.soulfulalchemist.com or inquire directly by emailing info@souldiveyoga.com.

4. Connect on Social Media

Follow Alex, *Soulful Alchemist,* on Instagram @alexsabbag
Stay in touch with Soul Dive Yoga on Instagram @souldiveyoga

About the Author

Alex Sabbag is an author, two-time business owner, and entrepreneur. She founded her most recent venture, Soul Dive Yoga, in 2022 in Palm Desert, California. Her personal story was forged from tragedy when her fiancé was diagnosed with terminal brain cancer in 2018. Seeking solace in the practice, she found healing and a profound mission to share the transformative power of yoga with the world. The Soul Dive space welcomes yogis of all levels to arrive just as they are for movement, breath and soulful connection.

In her book, *Soul Dive: My Journey into the Deep*, Alex shares her story of resilient triumph, in and outside the studio, on and off the yoga mat. Through her book and in her studio, she hopes to empower and inspire others to embrace life's challenges while finding greater peace and presence. She works to create a supportive community for people to gather free from judgment and expectation in a safe, welcoming and loving environment.

Alex is a contributor at Entrepreneur's Leadership Network and has been featured in Women's Health, The Desert Sun, Los Angeles Wire and NBC Palm Springs. To explore the offerings and ethos of Soul Dive Yoga, visit souldiveyoga.com.